LETHAL MEDICINE

Also by Harvey F. Wachsman

The American Law of Medical Malpractice
4 volumes (co-authored with Steven E. Pegalis)

LETHAL MEDICINE

THE EPIDEMIC OF MEDICAL MALPRACTICE IN AMERICA

HARVEY F. WACHSMAN, M.D., J.D.,

with Steven Alschuler

HENRY HOLT AND COMPANY • NEW YORK

Henry Holt and Company, Inc.
Publishers since 1866
115 West 18th Street
New York, New York 10011

Henry Holt® is a registered
trademark of Henry Holt and Company, Inc.

Library of Congress Cataloging-in-Publication Data
Wachsman, Harvey F.
Lethal medicine : the epidemic of medical malpractice in America /
by Harvey F. Wachsman with Steven Alschuler. — 1st ed.
p.   cm.
1. Physicians—Malpractice—United States.   I. Alschuler, Steven.
II. Title.
KF2905.3.W28   1993
346.7303'32—dc20   93-11324
[347.306332]   CIP

ISBN 0-8050-2513-8

Henry Holt books are available for special
promotions and premiums. For details contact:
Director, Special Markets.

First Edition—1993

Designed by Victoria Hartman

Printed in the United States of America
All first editions are printed on acid-free paper. ∞

1   3   5   7   9   10   8   6   4   2

This book is dedicated to the many honorable,
diligent, hardworking physicians who have dedicated
their lives to the service of the public,
physicians who save lives every day through their
tireless efforts, skill, and knowledge.

To my wife, Kathryn; to my children,
Ashley; Marea; Melissa; Dara; David; Jacqueline;
Lauren; and Derek; to my father, Ben;
and to the memory of my mother, Mollie.—H. F. W.

To Laurel, for her good advice and for
making everything worthwhile.—S. A.

CONTENTS

PREFACE

Medicine has been one of my great loves for most of my life. I can still remember reading Sinclair Lewis's *Arrowsmith* as a sophomore at Thomas Jefferson High School in Brooklyn and knowing right then and there that I wanted to become a doctor. At the time, for a kid from Bedford-Stuyvesant—the first in his family even to attend high school—this was easier said than done.

Though my parents and grandparents lacked formal schooling, they had never let that hold them back. My grandfather, who had had virtually no education, was an inventor and mathematician who held over 100 patents and was responsible for the first power-driven knitting machine. My father and mother both became successful businesspeople in their own right, but most important, they all had excellent, creative, inquisitive minds and they passed on to me their love of knowledge and their understanding of the value of hard work.

Thus there was no doubt in my mind that I would become a physician, and when I graduated from college and then medical school I went on to receive my training in neurosurgery and was fortunate enough to be able to fulfill my childhood dream.

Perhaps my background is what makes me feel as strongly as I do about medical malpractice. I know how hard it is to become a doctor and I understand how difficult a profession it can be. There is no profession more noble, none whose practitioners make more sacrifices. This book is dedicated to all physicians who earn the respect and esteem of their patients every day.

Negligent physicians, on the other hand, dishonor and discredit the entire medical profession. They do a disservice not only to the public but to all of those who have practiced diligently, who have spent all night in an operating room, who have devoted themselves—twenty-four hours a day, seven days a week—to their patients.

I received my introduction to medical malpractice almost at the very start of my career. While serving as chief resident in neurosurgery, an emergency case came into the hospital—a child who had been shot in the head. I operated on that boy for hours, virtually all night, and afterward in the recovery room I saw him moving his arms and legs purposefully—a sure sign that he was on his way to at least a potential recovery. That was a gratifying moment for a surgeon; it seemed that the operation had been a success. Sometime later, while I was seeing other patients elsewhere in the hospital, another doctor determined that the patient's blood level was low, not an uncommon occurrence following surgery. An anesthesiologist administered a transfusion, but gave the child too much blood. This foolish, sloppy error caused the patient to go into congestive heart failure and killed the boy.

On another occasion, in making routine rounds, I came across a patient who was obviously dead and cold, lying in a bed. I called for the nurse. No one knew what had happened. No one knew how long he'd been there. No one knew what had caused his death. I reprimanded the nursing staff for what I believed was negligence on its part and, though still upset, I went on with my rounds. One of the other patients I examined was a man with a broken neck who was quadriplegic, and whose body was being held in a Striker Frame, a device that allowed his paralyzed body to be moved more easily. Because of their paralysis, patients in this condition are always at risk of pulmonary emboli—blood clots that move from the leg to the heart and can result in death. But he was fine at that moment.

Several hours later, while on duty in the emergency room, I got a call from the nurse. They weren't sure, she said, and they didn't know why, but they thought this quadraplegic patient had expired. Hadn't anyone been monitoring him, I asked. Hadn't anyone been alert to the risks? How long had he been dead? No one was certain.

Late that night, after a stint in surgery, I got another surprise. I went on rounds, beginning at about 2:00 A.M. What did I find? Another patient lying dead and cold in bed. No one knew what had happened. There was a notation on his chart from hours earlier about his having eaten some cake from his dinner tray, but no notations since then. He had been dead for hours and no one had noticed.

Three patients in one day. Three individuals who died in their hospital beds, unattended and unnoticed except by accident. I can still remember my reaction. Working as hard as I was, I had little patience for nurses who were sloppy and careless. If they didn't even notice when a patient was dead, I asked, how could they be expected to care for patients who were alive?

At any rate, after about three or four years I began to realize that the demands of a medical career left little opportunity to pursue some of the other important interests I had. I had always been intrigued by public policy and was fascinated with the laws that govern our country. While still practicing medicine, I enrolled in law school in New York and continued seeing patients to earn my law school tuition.

My decision, after graduating and passing the bar, to specialize in medical malpractice litigation, was a natural one. At first, my wife Kathryn and I formed a partnership together, Wachsman & Wachsman, and began building a practice in Connecticut. After only a short time, however, I met my current partner, Steven Pegalis, and we decided to join forces. I eventually joined him in Great Neck, where we are still headquartered today, and our collaboration has proved to be a tremendous success. Today,

Pegalis & Wachsman is the largest law firm in the country representing victims of medical malpractice.

Steve Pegalis is an extraordinary human being. His intellect, his compassion, and his devotion to serving the public interest make him one of the finest trial lawyers in America, as well as one of my best friends and most trusted advisers.

In the years we have worked together we have had tens of thousands of people walk through our doors, some in despair over their own conditions, others grieving the loss of a loved one. These people are no different from millions of others in communities around the United States. They are like some of the people I just described—healthy one day, without a care in the world; the next day a victim of negligence, incompetence, or medical abuse.

We view our law practice much as I view this book: as a way of serving the public, of helping people who have been hurt and, it is hoped, of protecting others from the same fate. As you will see in the pages that follow, the American public needs all the protection it can get.

—Harvey F. Wachsman, M.D., J.D.
Great Neck, New York

AUTHOR'S NOTE

This book contains descriptions of numerous cases of medical malpractice—cases in which patients became victims of physician negligence. All of these case histories are true. Most of them, particularly those described in depth, are ones in which the author was personally involved. Many of the names of people involved in these cases, along with some minor details about their lives, have been altered for legal reasons. However, all of the relevant information about the care these patients received and the injuries (or worse) they suffered is accurate.

1

THE PUBLIC AT RISK

A ndy Phillips hadn't been feeling well for several days. He assumed it was the flu or some intestinal virus, and the aches and occasional nausea were nothing he couldn't live with for a few days. All week at work—he held a middle-management position with a *Fortune* 500 corporation—he continued to function normally, remaining as active as usual despite his mild illness. It was now Friday afternoon and Mr. Phillips was thinking about the Little League game his son's team had scheduled for the weekend. He didn't know if he'd be able to make it. He decided that he ought to see a doctor and, since his own family doctor wouldn't be around late on a Friday, he stopped off at the hospital emergency room on his way home from work.

By the time he arrived at the hospital that Friday evening, Mr. Phillips was beginning to feel worse—a little light-headed and increasingly nauseous. He had some difficulty retaining his balance when he walked through the waiting area to the nurse's station. As he stood at her desk, the nurse took down a cursory medical history and asked him to fill out the usual insurance forms. There were no chairs nearby, so he remained standing as he worked on the forms.

Andy Phillips's mind wandered to the plans for his son Joey's game. He hoped that the doctors could prescribe some medication, and that with a good night's sleep, he would feel better.

But soon Mr. Phillips's queasiness and light-headedness turned to dizziness. He fell to the floor and hit his head. He was going to miss that Little League game, all right. And he was going to miss a lot more.

The treatment he received in the hours that followed—in the local hospital he was so familiar with—was characterized by negligence and ineptitude. By doing what he thought was the sensible thing—going to the hospital when he felt sick—Andy Phillips set off a chain of events that destroyed his life.

When Andy Phillips fell and hit his head, he also had a seizure, an important medical point indicating possible neurological injury. The nurse made a note of this seizure on his chart. But when the emergency room resident examined him, he ignored that notation and decided, based on Phillips's prior dizziness and some redness he discovered around one of his ears, that the patient was suffering from a middle-ear infection. The doctor apparently never considered the possibility of a head injury and never ordered an X-ray.

Instead, he treated the patient for an ear infection and injected him with Demerol for the pain. Painkillers like Demerol are exactly the wrong treatment for someone with a head injury because they mask symptoms. As a result, no one in this busy emergency room saw any problem until someone on staff finally noticed that, after eight hours of lying there under sedation, Phillips was unconscious and had become paralyzed on his entire left side.

By now, most laypeople would wonder whether Andy Phillips might have suffered a head injury from the fall in the emergency room. But no one in the emergency room that night even considered it. Fixated on the redness around his ear and ignoring the earlier seizure, these professionals jumped to the conclusion that the middle-ear infection they diagnosed initially must have spread to the brain. On that basis, they put Mr. Phillips into an ambulance and sent him to the nearest hospital with a qualified neuro-surgeon on staff—which, unfortunately for Mr. Phillips, was about eighty miles away.

At this second hospital, the neurosurgeon immediately ordered an X-ray of the patient's skull and found that virtually every prior step in the diagnosis and treatment had been terribly wrong. There was no middle-ear infection; Phillips's dizziness had been caused by his upset stomach. When he fell and hit his head, the impact had cracked his skull. The redness around his ear, which was central to the first doctor's diagnosis, was just a bruise from the fall. The Demerol he had been given actually confused the issue, preventing his true neurological condition from being determined during those critical hours.

The neurosurgeon performed emergency surgery to remove an epidural hemotoma (bleeding on the brain) and part of the skull—surgery which should have been performed hours earlier. Had this head injury been diagnosed accurately at first, Andy Phillips would most likely be fine today.

Instead, this once happily married, twenty-six-year-old father of two, with a promising career and a bright future, is irreparably brain-damaged. He has lost his job and his home. As neither he nor his wife was able to cope with their marriage under the cir-cumstances, it soon dissolved. Andy Phillips now lives with his mother and spends most of his time watching children's shows on television. He particularly likes "Sesame Street." And all he had was an upset stomach.

Of course, the irony of this case is that if Phillips had simply been given a chair to sit in while he filled out his insurance forms at the nurse's station in the emergency room, he would not have fallen in the first place and none of the ensuing events would have transpired.

Like most Americans, Andy Phillips never imagined that he could become a victim of medical malpractice. But the ordeal of misdi-agnosis, mistreatment, and neglect that he suffered—a process that turned an upset stomach into irreparable brain damage and permanent paralysis—is merely one of innumerable horrors physicians inflict on patients every day.

More than 100,000 deaths a year, and hundreds of thousands of injuries, are caused by medical malpractice in American hospitals. In recent years, when the United States considered going to war in the Persian Gulf, there was intense debate in Congress, in the media, and on Main Streets everywhere concerning the potential loss of life among the military. When our country is beset by a horrible epidemic like AIDS, we expend vast resources and engage in open and well-publicized discussions of the issues involved. Yet there has never been such a discussion about the epidemic of medical malpractice—an epidemic that claims 100,000 lives a year—and almost no public resources have been devoted to its study or eradication.

While we should hardly diminish our interest in or the fervor of our debate over these other crucial matters, we should once and for all disclose the well-kept medical secret: Twice as many people in this country die each year as a result of medical malpractice than died during the entire Vietnam War. Twice as many Americans die at the hands of their physicians than in accidents on our nation's roadways.

Physicians since the time of Hippocrates have taken oaths to protect and heal their patients, never to harm or injure them through negligence. But the fact is that some doctors do a lot of harm. The American public may take the Hippocratic Oath to heart—along with medical society standards and state licensing requirements—but the sad truth is that physicians in this country have injured or killed millions of people over the years, and this epidemic continues unabated.

While this may be news to the American public, it is certainly nothing new. Medical malpractice has been a factor throughout the history of the medical profession. There have always been incompetent, negligent, even evil doctors, just as there have always been such practitioners in other professions. Tales of the Roman emperors 2,000 years ago tell of conspiracies in which the royal physicians played a key role, either by failing to treat an emperor who'd been poisoned by his enemies or by actually pre-scribing medication that would kill.

In the United States, some of the most important figures in our history have been victims of poor medical care, including our first President, George Washington, who was bled to death by his doc-tors in a misguided effort to treat the pneumonia he contracted in his old age.

When President James Garfield was shot by an assassin in 1881, he survived the shooting and would likely have lived a long life if not for a ridiculously botched surgical effort. While walking through the train station in Washington, D.C. (the site on which the National Gallery of Art is now located), President Garfield was shot by Charles Guiteau, who fired two 44-caliber bullets into the president's body. The bullets, though fired at close range, had not damaged any of Garfield's vital organs. But surgery, which was far more risky then than it is today, should have been avoided com-pletely. Nevertheless the president's doctors were determined to locate and extract the bullets.

Alexander Graham Bell, the inventor, designed a special metal detector to be used by President Garfield's surgeons to locate the bullet. With the president lying on his bed, the physicians held the metal detector over him and, of course, it indicated the presence of metal. They cut into his body at that location. No bullet. They moved the detector. Again, it indicated metal. Again, they cut. Again, nothing. What these brilliant doctors couldn't figure out was that the president was lying on a bed with metal springs beneath him. Bell's machine couldn't tell the difference between the metal in the bullets and the metal of the bedsprings. The detector kept indicating the presence of metal, and the surgeons kept digging into the body, making one hole after another and reaching into the president's body with their unsterilized fingers. They never did find the bullets (which was irrelevant to the president's treatment in any event), but they created so many holes as they probed with their unsanitary hands that the onset of sepsis (infection), which ulti-mately caused the president's death, was inevitable.

■ ■ ■

A great deal has changed since President Garfield's day, but despite more than a century of scientific advances, medical malpractice today is as serious a problem as it has ever been. Most of the time it happens under a cloak of secrecy. While certain horror stories occasionally come to light in local media, these generally are treated as the exceptions rather than the commonplace occurrences they are. The fact is that only a tiny percentage of all the incidents of incompetence and negligence ever comes to light, and the medical community and the government officials charged with policing the profession refuse even to acknowledge the problem. The result is a grave lack of understanding among all segments of our society—government, the legal and medical professions, and the general public—of the broad scope of the malpractice epidemic.

Lucian L. Leape, a surgeon and lecturer at the Harvard School of Public Health, recently told the American Association for the Advancement of Science that: "Medical injury is indeed a hidden epidemic. . . . It's time for the medical profession to become as concerned about safety as about cure." He estimated that approximately 1 in 400 hospitalized patients die each year—100,000 deaths—and nearly 1 in 25—more than a million Americans—are injured as a result of their medical treatment.

Medical malpractice has become a plague in America. The fact is that a trip to the doctor can pose risks—risks that we all need to be prepared for and protected against.

From the moment we're born—indeed, from almost the time of conception—we are in the hands of physicians. They counsel the expectant mother during her pregnancy and then bring the child into the world. It's hard not to think well of doctors. Like members of the clergy, it seems as if they're the ones who are always there when we need them. One of our first thoughts in times of crisis is getting to a doctor or a hospital, and rightly so. Through a combination of science and technology, skill, experience, and education, physicians cure diseases and deal with problems every day that the average person finds intimidating and unfathomable.

Most of the time, most physicians do fabulous work, and they truly do deserve a special place in our hearts and minds. This is a profession that requires years of education—a lifetime of education, really. Those doctors who give up their personal lives, who devote all of their skills and energies to their patients, deserve society's gratitude.

Most of the time, when a patient dies or is crippled through illness it is not malpractice. In many cases, the tragic result could not have been averted, no matter what the doctors had done. But when avoidable mistakes are made in the treatment of a patient— when they are caused by sloppiness, negligence, ignorance, arrogance, or just plain bad medical care—and when they result in death or serious injury, that's malpractice. And it's inexcusable. We extend a great deal of trust to members of the medical profession and, as a result, its practitioners bear an especially heavy responsibility.

We assume that the physician is acting in our best interests. We assume that doctors are highly educated, so they must know more than we do. We assume that doctors' licenses are a certification of their competency. We assume that prestigious medical centers would never allow incompetent physicians to practice there. And finally we assume that if they weren't competent, we'd all know about it, and someone would do something to stop them from practicing. More often than most people realize, these assumptions are terribly wrong.

Unfortunately, the truth is that there *are* bad doctors, more than are ever acknowledged. Medical malpractice is not uncommon. According to some reports, at least 5 percent of the nation's doctors are considered by medical authorities to be unfit to practice. These physicians may account for tens of thousands of needless injuries and deaths each year because of unnecessary operations, botched procedures, faulty drug prescriptions, and inept diagnoses and treatments.

In thirty-two years as a public school teacher, Rita Dole had rarely taken a sick day. In recent years, since her husband passed away, she had been particularly dedicated to her work. It was more than just something to keep her busy. Her students reminded her of her own children in their youth, and the responsibility she felt for them gave her a sense of purpose.

An occasion arose when she did take a few days off, however. After a week of suffering from a fever, stomach cramps, and a general loss of energy, she contacted Dr. Gerald Litman, a local general practitioner, who was able to see her that same day. In the course of describing her medical history to the doctor, Dole told him that her sister had died of ovarian cancer and her mother of cancer of the mouth. This family propensity had always worried her and she wanted to be sure the doctor was aware of it.

Dr. Litman examined her and took a sample of her stool. He asked her about her eating habits, and she told him that a few days prior to becoming ill, she had eaten some ice cream bars. That was probably the problem, Dr. Litman said. She was experiencing lactose intolerance, a condition which causes the body to react negatively to dairy products. He told her not to worry, to go home and rest, and that he would contact her if the lab results showed anything unusual. She did not hear from the doctor and assumed everything would be all right as long as she stayed away from those ice cream bars.

Over the next eighteen months, Rita Dole continued to experience occasional nausea and cramps, but she didn't think anything of it. Dr. Litman had explained that these symptoms might appear from time to time if she ate milk or cheese products. As a result, any time she felt ill she assumed it was something she had eaten.

One day, however, she noticed blood in her stool, and she became concerned. She immediately contacted Dr. Litman, who referred her to Dr. Harvey Mandel, a gastroenterologist, for further evaluation.

At this point, Ms. Dole was fifty-six years old. She had been experiencing abdominal pain for eighteen months. She had a family history of cancer. Most important, she had bleeding from her rectum—a symptom that cannot be ignored. Bleeding is a sign that something is seriously wrong. And the doctor's job is to find out what is causing it. This patient had all the symptoms of colon cancer. As a matter of fact, in cases like this one cancer should be the doctor's first assumption, and it should be investigated until it is ruled out as the cause of the illness.

Dr. Mandel examined Rita Dole and determined that, indeed, there was blood in her stool. But rather than probing further, he attributed her continued illness to irritable bowel syndrome, a minor stomach ailment with no significant consequences. He told her that she was fine, that she looked wonderful, and that she should stay away from ice cream and other milk products and take Metamucil, an over-the-counter laxative. Her bleeding, he said, was probably being caused by some hemorrhoids, although he had been unable actually to locate them. He sent her home with some pamphlets describing irritable bowel syndrome and told her she had nothing to worry about.

Rita Dole began to feel a little better and, although she continued to have attacks of nausea and stomach discomfort, she assumed it was nothing. After all, two doctors had told her so.

But about six months later—two years after she originally complained about her illness to Dr. Litman—the bleeding returned and she suffered an unbearable attack of cramps, nausea, and stomach pain. She had constant diarrhea and frequent vomiting. At this point, she finally discussed her problem with her son, a pediatrician, who examined her personally and felt a lump in her abdomen. He immediately referred her for further tests—a sonogram, an MRI, and a colonoscopy—all of which should have been performed two years earlier, as a matter of routine medical practice.

When the appropriate tests were finally performed, colon cancer was discovered. But by this time it was in an advanced stage, completely penetrating the bowel wall and involving the lymph nodes to a significant degree. Had the proper tests been conducted at the outset, and had the cancer been diagnosed and removed at that time, Rita Dole would likely have had a long life ahead of her. Cancer of the colon, detected at an early stage, has a cure rate of approximately 80 percent.

By the time surgery was performed, however, it was clear that the patient was terminal. Her son contacted us a short time later, obviously outraged at the negligent physicians who had ignored his mother's cancer for two years—physicians who were either too lazy or too incompetent to conduct a proper examination, who attributed two years of abdominal pain and vomiting to an imagined inability to digest dairy products, who convinced their patient that her rectal bleeding was due to nonexistent hemorrhoids. We filed suit on behalf of Rita Dole and her son. Not surprisingly, the doctors' insurance companies paid a settlement without requiring us to go to trial. Unfortunately, Rita Dole did not live long enough to see it.

Malpractice can happen anywhere, to patients from all walks of life in every part of this country, whether it be in a small clinic in a rural area or in the emergency room of a major metropolitan medical center. That no one talks about it makes it all the more incredible. How is it possible that this epidemic can exist in a modern, open society like ours? How can there be so many bad doctors out there? With this country's system of education, the medical profession should have the very best minds we produce. How then can medical incompetence exist on so widespread a basis?

Several years ago, the president of the American Medical Association, who would be expected to support the position of physicians, offered this view:

> It's said that about half of medical knowledge is outdated every ten years. If that is true, then a doctor who has not taken any postgraduate courses since he left medical school [could] really be practicing back in the Dark Ages.
>
> This is why the American Medical Association urges a program of continuing education to upgrade a physician's competence. . . . We feel about a third are real, honest to goodness participants in this program. The other two-thirds is the group we have to get at.

Those other two-thirds, whether the AMA "gets to" them or not, will continue to practice medicine.

While even the AMA acknowledges the existence of a problem, the discussion of medical malpractice is generally limited to trade publications and professional journals. As far as the general public is concerned, most people can find out more about a car they plan to buy than they can about a doctor who may hold their life in his or her hand.

A study conducted by the California Medical Association published in 1977 found that in one year alone, 24,000 patients in California hospitals "had an adverse outcome that appeared to be the fault of one or more health care providers and for which the patient would be successful in litigation."

Another study, conducted in 1990 for the New York State Department of Health by a team from Harvard University, contains findings that are similarly shocking and that generally support the evidence we see in our legal practice every day. While the Harvard team has disseminated its findings among various medical publications, this information rarely finds its way into the mainstream media, where the public would have greater access to it.

The Harvard study analyzed more than 30,000 sets of medical records, selected at random from hospitals in New York State, and researchers studied two types of medical mishaps in depth: adverse events and negligent events. Adverse events are medical errors that could have been prevented, but for which there was no clear evidence that the doctor was at fault. These could include incidents as simple as prescribing medication to which a patient had a serious allergic reaction.

The second category, negligence, involves incidents in which the physician did not live up to the normally expected standard of care. These are cases of medical malpractice, in which a patient suffers, and it is clear that the doctor should have known better and performed differently.

The Harvard findings are staggering. More than 98,000 patients in hospitals in New York State alone, in a single year, were victims of adverse events. Applied to the population of the entire country, this rate of medical error would give us a total of approximately 2 million patients a year unnecessarily injured or killed in hospitals across America.

Twenty-seven percent of the injuries—a large percentage of them serious and permanent, affecting nearly 27,000 New York hospital patients—were caused by negligence, according to the Harvard report. Sixty-six hundred of those incidents resulted in death. In fact, the more serious the injury, the more likely it was to have been a result of medical malpractice.

These findings are consistent with those of the earlier California study, which, though using different methodology, documented the same degree of medical error in faulty procedures, incomplete diagnosis, and incorrect treatment, and a similar array of resulting disabilities. As in New York State, a large percentage of the California fatalities studied were caused by medical negligence. And in general, the greater the disability, the greater the likelihood of negligence.

Speaking to situations like the one experienced by Andy Phillips, the authors of the Harvard study found an alarmingly high rate of medical errors in emergency rooms and attributed the vast majority of them to negligence:

> The high rate of negligence in adverse events resulting from treatment in the emergency room could be caused by several factors. . . . Emergency rooms are sometimes staffed with part-time physicians who are not well trained in emergency care. Because they are frequently very busy, these physicians have less time to spend with each patient. Finally, some of the sickest patients enter the hospital through the emergency room.

The Harvard study also showed that for:

> 58 percent of patients with severe trauma treated in the emergency room there had been serious errors in treatment. Although many of these errors involved mistakes or delays in diagnosis, most were errors in treatment. The risk of error was increased with certain characteristics of the patient, such as alcoholism and the presence of multiple injuries, but the investigators concluded that the treating physician's inexperience was the chief cause of the high rate of error.

Citing statistics that sound like they were written to describe the Phillips case, the Harvard study found that "adverse events resulting from errors in diagnosis and in non-invasive treatment were judged to be due to negligence in over three-fourths of patients. Falls were considered due to negligence in 45 percent of the instances."

Apparently, these researchers have found cases of medical malpractice happening in emergency rooms all the time. This particular venue, where hospitals deal with the most seriously ill patients, along with some routine ailments, is staffed by the least trained, least experienced, and most overworked physicians in the hospital. As a result, diagnosis and treatment suffer. And sometimes, the type of standard precautions that would prevent accidents, like Andy Phillips's fall, are simply overlooked.

The Harvard and California studies are more thorough than anything else that has been done on this subject, yet their results, and those of other studies conducted over the years, are surprising only because of how little attention has been paid to them. As long ago as 1976, for example, the Malpractice Commission of the U.S. Department of Health, Education and Welfare found that a large percentage of injuries that occurred to patients in hospitals resulted from medical negligence. The director of the commission estimated that 14.5 percent of injuries to these patients were due to negligence.

These statistics provide scientific documentation of what we have been saying for years as a result of our own observation. The studies strongly support the contention of public advocacy groups and other experts that more than 100,000 deaths a year—and more than 500,000 serious injuries—are caused by malpractice in hospitals around the United States. And these conservative statistics don't begin to account for the untold number of deaths and injuries that take place quietly, in doctors' offices and free-standing clinics. But they do provide sufficient evidence of the pitfalls Americans face in their effort to obtain competent care from some physicians.

We are all at risk. This epidemic cuts across all ages, races, sexes, and economic groups. Incompetent and negligent physicians come in all shapes and sizes, practicing in virtually every specialty. Of course, the most vulnerable among us face the worst odds— the old, the poor, members of minority groups are victimized at higher rates than others. Research continually finds that minorities receive lower quality health care in general, as do the indigent and uninsured population. For these groups, as well as for senior citizens, the rate of medical malpractice is higher as well.

But don't think that you are only at risk if you use overcrowded municipal hospitals in poverty-stricken neighborhoods of our inner cities. That's probably what Ann Marie Hanks thought. A single mother of two boys—Danny, eleven, and John, thirteen— Ms. Hanks was living a blissfully normal life in a well-off community in the suburbs. Though not a wealthy woman by any means, she always did what she could to make sure that her sons had the best of everything. That included their medical care. When they needed to have several baby teeth removed in order to continue with their orthodontia, she received referrals—three recommendations from local dentists, in fact—to someone she thought was an excellent oral surgeon, Dr. Joanne Leno.

At 8:15 A.M. one Saturday morning, Ann Hanks took Danny and John to Dr. Leno's office, located in a small suburban office center. John needed to have four teeth pulled and he was a little frightened, but his mother reassured him that Dr. Leno was the best and that there was absolutely nothing to worry about. They were accompanied by Peter Balleri, a family friend who happened also to be a police officer. Dr. Leno was not yet at the office when they arrived.

On checking with the receptionist, Ms. Hanks was told that the doctor was not yet in the office, but that her assistant would begin to prepare the boys. There was some confusion, however, over what sedative they were to be given, and the mother insisted that the receptionist call Dr. Leno at home to clarify the instructions. This was of particular concern to Ann Hanks because John was afraid of needles and she had hoped to spare him that anxiety. After a phone call to the doctor it was finally agreed that Noctec, a chloral hydrate sedative, would be administered orally. Ms. Hanks was reassured that "we give Noctec all the time; it will just make them groggy like they were drunk."

While Ann Hanks remained in the reception area filling out forms, Peter Balleri accompanied the boys back to a treatment room with one of Dr. Leno's assistants. The assistant measured out half a plastic cup full for Danny and a full cup—approximately 12 teaspoons—for John. Danny drank his dosage quickly, but John was reluctant. He didn't like to take medicine. But Peter Balleri and John's younger brother finally talked him into it.

The boys were brought into separate treatment rooms and, as Dr. Leno had now arrived, she began to work on the older boy. Mr. Balleri left the room, but let the doctor know that he would be right outside the door, in the event that John became disturbed and needed him. Following is the statement he made later describing what happened:

"I heard John moaning, as if he were in pain and I heard the doctor tell John in a rather loud terse voice, 'John calm down, behave, there are three down and one to go.' I then heard the doctor say, 'John calm down, behave, breathe, breathe deeply, behave yourself.' I walked over to the receptionist and asked if the doctor knew I was here to help and if she would call me. She said, 'The doctor knows. If she needs you she'll call.'

"I walked back to the treatment door and just then it swung open and one of the assistants rushed out and into a third treatment room at the end of the hall. This was about five to eight minutes after I heard the doctor tell John to breathe. I asked if everything was okay, and she replied very quickly 'Everything is okay, don't worry, we have everything under control.' I knew she was not telling the truth.

"She found what she was looking for in that room, which I later learned was a pulseoximeter [a device that reads the pulse and determines how much oxygen is being received by the body's tissue], and then rushed past me and back into the treatment room where John was. As I followed her, and before she closed the door, I saw John in the treatment chair in a semi-seated position with blood all over the front of his shirt. I remained outside the door for another twelve to fifteen minutes when again the door swung open and an assistant came rushing out of the room with a look of terror on her face. She said 'You'd better go in. We need help. We need help.'

"I immediately went into the room and observed the doctor standing at the right side of John, who I felt, based on my experience as a police officer, was dead.

"She was just looking at him not doing anything and she in an hysterical voice yelled, 'I can't find a pulse, find a pulse, help find a pulse.' I felt for the carotid artery. Nothing. I then tried both wrists. Nothing. I then ripped up John's shirt and put my ear to his chest and there was no heartbeat.

"By this time the doctor was pounding on John's collarbone with the bottom of her right fist. I realized that she was trying to give CPR, or what she thought was CPR, but with John almost sitting up, his chin down on his chest, there was no open airway and she wasn't even close to his heart. I moved her aside, yelled at her to lower the chair flat and I began chest compressions. I asked her if she had a resuscitator. She said no. She began putting an ordinary oxygen mask over John's mouth and I had to tell her that if it didn't force air in, it was no good. She turned to one of her assistants and said 'Call an ambulance.'

"While I continued CPR, the doctor began roughly forcing a suction device down John's throat. I yelled at her that she was going to injure his throat, that she had to breathe in, not suction out.

"By this time, the police arrived and the officers and I lifted John from the chair to the floor and a policeman began giving CPR while another administered oxygen.

"Ann Marie [who had remained in the reception area up until this point] was now in the hall. The ambulance arrived and John was transported to the hospital and eventually pronounced dead."

In a case that is illustrative of the type of risk that all medical consumers face, the Hanks family took for granted what they thought was going to be a routine trip to the dentist. John was given an overdose of chloral hydrate (Noctec) by an untrained office assistant. The doctor, who should have administered the drug herself, was not even present at the time. Nor did she bother to monitor the child's heart rate during the procedure—a routine precaution under the circumstances. Dr. Leno did not know how to use an endotracheal tube to open an airway. She never made use of a crash cart (containing oxygen, an endotracheal tube, various drugs, and equipment necessary to resuscitate a patient) only a few feet away in her office, and apparently didn't even realize that it was there. There is also some reason to believe that Dr. Leno may have continued trying to extract John's teeth for some time after his heart had stopped.

Shortly after her son's death, Ann Hanks received an anonymous letter from a former employee of Dr. Leno's, describing the substandard care she had seen in that office every day. While none of the assistants was medically trained, she said, they all wore nurse's uniforms and regularly administered sedatives, assisted during surgery, and monitored patients' vital signs. Dr. Leno was always late, always overbooked, and never able to take sufficient time with each patient.

Despite the county medical examiner's finding that the death was caused by the "administration of an apparently excessive dosage of chloral hydrate," Dr. Leno has denied any wrongdoing. Her defense in this case, which is currently in suit, is that John had heart problems to begin with and that they had caused his death, not an overdose. This came as something of a surprise to John's family, since he had never been diagnosed as having a heart ailment or any other serious illness. He had always been a particularly active child, very athletic, participating in sports at school and with his friends in the neighborhood.

Dr. Leno has thus far offered no defense for what happened to Danny Hanks, John's eleven-year-old little brother, who helped persuade John to take his medication. Danny, who was waiting his turn in the next treatment room during this episode, remained in bed for more than a day, sleeping off the effects of the drug.

■ ■ ■

The malpractice cases we describe here are more than just isolated incidents attributable to a few bad doctors. In fact, there is a good chance that you or someone you know may be receiving treatment from a physician who has, at some time, committed malpractice. There are those who have attributed the malpractice problem to a small number of incompetent physicians who have injured a large number of patients. But the Harvard study mentioned earlier analyzed malpractice claims to see whether this hypothesis was accurate. What the researchers found, in coming to the conclusion that "clearly modern medicine is a risky enterprise," was that, in fact, the fault lies with a substantial portion of the profession: "Momentary, inadvertant mistakes can be made by even the most careful and concerned doctors, just as by their counterparts in any other walk of life. But when a doctor makes a mistake, the unfortunate result is that a patient may be hurt, often severely. . . ."

As one of the Harvard researchers, Troyen A. Brendan, M.D., of Brigham and Women's Hospital in Boston has said: "This isn't a problem of a couple of bad apples, but rather something happening at the hospital level. There's a lot of substandard care in hospitals in the United States."

Often, it seems as if that substandard care is almost impossible to avoid. So it was with Harold Schneider, an advertising executive on his way home from work, who became another statistic in this nightmare of medical incompetence. As in so many other cases, mistakes were made from the outset, then repeated and compounded in a horrifying sequence that shattered Mr. Schneider's body and his life.

Harold Schneider left the office at 5:00 P.M. and soon entered onto the expressway homeward. The traffic was congested, but moving. Suddenly, the car in front of him stopped short. He hit his brakes in time, but the driver in back of him didn't. Mr. Schneider's car was hit from the rear and crushed between the two vehicles.

When the police and the paramedics arrived at the scene, they found Schneider unconscious. Using the mechanical prying device known as "the jaws of life," they pulled apart the body of the crushed car and carefully removed its driver into the waiting ambulance. By the time they arrived at a nearby hospital, Schneider had regained consciousness. He was immediately examined by a staff neurologist, Dr. Lee Hai, who noticed that the patient's eyes were slightly crossed. It was on the basis of that one "sign" that Dr. Hai arrived at his diagnosis: a brain stem contusion (bruise). That diagnosis was absolutely wrong.

With a brain stem contusion, the patient would have been unconscious. And while Mr. Schneider may have been unconscious at the scene of the accident, he was awake when the doctor examined him. Also, if Dr. Hai's diagnosis had been correct, one side of the patient's face would have been paralyzed. It would be impossible for a brain stem contusion to affect the eye, as the doctor thought it had, without also affecting the facial muscles. But there was no such paralysis evident here. The slightly crossed eyes that seemed so important to Dr. Hai had absolutely nothing to do with this accident. Had he taken the trouble to ask his patient, the doctor would have found out that they were nothing more than a lifelong condition that had never caused any problem.

On his arrival at the hospital, and consistently for the next few days, the patient complained of back pain. Contusions were found on his back. He had trouble swallowing, and an examination found contusions of his esophagus as well. Contusions on the back and esophagus. Back pain and trouble swallowing. Anyone with an elementary understanding of human anatomy would look at the one part of the body located between the back and the esophagus—the vertebrae, or spine. The symptoms were crying out for such an examination, and all that was needed was an X-ray.

Dr. Hai discharged Harold Schneider after a few days in the hospital. No X-rays of the spine were taken and no complete neurological examination was conducted. A month later, still in some pain and having trouble walking, Schneider returned to the same hospital and was ordered to undergo a program of physical rehabilitation, including a regimen of deep knee bends. When he was first admitted for this program, a notation was made in his chart that he was able to do twenty deep knee bends. By the time he left the hospital some weeks later, he needed two canes and assistance from two attendants just to walk.

By now, Harold Schneider wanted to escape the cold weather and visit his mother in Florida, assuming that she could help care for him during his rehabilitation. Dr. Hai recommended that he take an exercycle with him on his trip, and sent him on his way without referring him to a local physician.

Schneider arrived in Florida with his legs continually getting weaker. His mother located a neurosurgeon in the area, who Schneider visited. But when he arrived at the doctor's office, the patient was so weak he couldn't even get himself onto the examining table. So the doctor didn't examine him. He sent Schneider home, where his condition continued to deteriorate.

After a time, the patient's mother contacted this physician again and expressed her continued concern. The neurosurgeon contacted Dr. Hai, and was informed about the initial diagnosis of a brain stem contusion. By phone, without bothering to see Schneider again, the local physician ordered a CAT scan of the patient's head. Of course, the CAT scan showed nothing since there never was any brain stem contusion.

Two months later, at home alone in his mother's mobile home, Harold Schneider collapsed on the floor, helpless and totally incapacitated. When his mother found him, she immediately called an ambulance and rushed him to a nearby hospital. There, for the first time—ten months after that initial automobile accident—X-rays were taken of Schneider's back and a proper neurological examination was performed. The results showed what should have been obvious all along: a compressed fracture of the vertebrae and a calcified disk. During the extended time that had passed, however, the calcified disk had been pressing against the spinal cord, wearing it down to the size of a thin ribbon.

Had surgery been done shortly after the accident, the prognosis for recovery would have been excellent. Performed ten months later, there was little that could be done. Harold Schneider would never walk again. The abominable course of treatment ordered by this succession of incompetent neurologists—the exercise and physical rehabilitation—was inhuman. It caused the patient months of pain and did irreparable damage to his body.

How did this tragedy happen? A chance automobile accident. An incompetent physician in charge of the case. It was an emergency case, where the patient felt his only choice was to put himself in the hands of the doctor present. A ridiculous diagnosis based on a simple condition—slightly crossed eyes—that Schneider had had for years. In scientific terms, the Harvard study described just this type of occurrence: "Diagnostic errors . . . were more likely to be judged negligent, and to result in serious disability." In nonmedical terminology, this patient never has a chance.

The epilogue to this story is perhaps most appalling. Some time after our firm brought a lawsuit and won a major settlement, we saw Dr. Hai again in another case of misdiagnosis. Again, it was unbelievable mistreatment and another patient destroyed. We sued again and won again. Our client received a substantial sum, but it was small solace, given his pain. What became of Dr. Hai? He moved to California and put up his shingle there.

Medical errors and medical malpractice can happen anywhere, at any stage in a patient's treatment, for any ailment. Whether in an emergency room or an operating room, a labor room or a delivery room, a patient's room or a doctor's office, patients can fall victim to botched procedures, inadequate monitoring, medical neglect, misdiagnosis, and mistreatment.

As you can see from the examples we've cited, it's all avoidable. "While many of the adverse events we found, such as drug reactions, are not preventable with current knowledge, many others are," the Harvard study team stated:

> Some of the adverse events we have identified could be prevented by better dissemination of information and establishment of protocols and guidelines for care. Our evidence suggests that this would be especially so for care given in the

emergency room. Other adverse events represent an educational, and in some cases, psychological challenge: how to effectively alter physician behavior.

That's really the key: Alter physicians' behavior and change their attitudes, so that malpractice happens less frequently, and so that when it does happen, it's dealt with quickly, not covered up to protect the doctor.

The first step in altering physician behavior undoubtedly is to get the profession to acknowledge the problem. Unfortunately, members of the medical profession would likely argue that we're exaggerating here, that we're worrying the public for no reason. They would say that malpractice occurs in only a few cases, and when it does happen no one feels worse about it than the doctor. But the statistics reveal the truth. It's not that malpractice rarely happens, it's that it's rarely reported. It's not that physicians are never negligent or incompetent, it's that negligence and incompetence are generally ignored. As we show in the chapters that follow, doctors rarely report the misconduct of other doctors. Medical societies, which are supposed to set standards for the profession, turn a blind eye, saying that it's not their job to discipline their members. State licensing boards, whose job that clearly is, say that they are understaffed and lack the resources to police physicians effectively. So thousands of incompetent doctors go about their business unimpeded and unpunished. As we describe, even when the most outrageous abuses occur—when physicians commit gross malpractice, then lie about it, perjure themselves, forge medical records, and destroy evidence—the perpetrators are rarely punished or even exposed.

Apparently, no one feels it's particularly important to let patients know about problem doctors. No one gives people an opportunity to protect themselves. Still, with all this evidence most people find it hard to accept the idea that medical malpractice could happen to them. It's not something they want to think about.

But consider the potential consequences, and think about all the choices we make every day. When we hire a contractor to repair our homes, we worry about whether he is competent and reliable. Shouldn't we have access to the information we need to make a informed decision about our medical care? What happened to Andy Phillips, Rita Dole, John Hanks, and Harold Schneider happens to people all across America, all the time. In the chapters that follow we tell you about some of these unfortunate victims. As you're reading, try to remember that we are all prospective patients. It is highly likely that you or someone close to you will have to spend some time in a hospital. When that time comes, you want to know what you or your loved one are up against.

2

MALPRACTICE BEYOND A DOUBT

Professional medical organizations and other advocates for doctors would have you believe that malpractice often involves differences of opinion, honest errors in judgment, second-guessing of physicians after the fact. Not only does our experience with thousands of cases of abuse, neglect, and ineptitude belie that claim but, as a matter of fact, the law does not allow for it. Courts have upheld for the past century the legal principle that doctors should not be second-guessed. If after examining a patient carefully and competently, the physician does what he or she thinks is best, the doctor cannot be liable for malpractice, even if that judgment turns out to have been wrong.

The American Medical Association is very good at doing surveys and reporting statistics. On some subjects it is a valuable source of information. But the statistics the association doesn't bother to compile would show that approximately 70 percent of all malpractice lawsuits involve the type of slip-up that would be obvious to even a first-year medical student. These lawsuits involve either (1) a failure by the doctor to be present when needed, (2) a failure to take an adequate medical history, or (3) a failure to perform an adequate examination. Often these failings result in misdiagnoses, delays in treatment, or mistreatments that can have severe consequences. Whether a physician is a pediatrician, a surgeon, a neurologist, an internist, or an anaesthesiologist—or practices in any other specialty—he or she cannot simply disregard the basics of good medicine. The type of lapses we see on a regular basis—not honest errors in judgment—are things most people would think could never happen.

Patients are not the only ones who should be concerned. Physicians should also, not only if they are to avoid malpractice suits but if they want to provide the best care possible. Some members of the medical profession may honestly believe that malpractice lawsuits are the fabrications of greedy lawyers. If they do, it is only because they have not focused on the way some of their colleagues practice medicine. Indeed, among these normally decent, honorable, hardworking physicians may be some who have treated their patients negligently without even thinking about it. They may simply have been fortunate enough not to have done any damage. But concern about negligence in the medical profession can benefit physicians in ways they rarely consider. All doctors and their families are patients at some point in their lives. They have as much at stake as anyone else in ensuring that incompetents are weeded out and that all physicians care for their patients diligently.

Clearly, when we describe cases of negligence we're not talking about unavoidable errors in treatment that are bound to occur on occasion. For example, if a physician diagnoses an infection in a patient, and believes that an antibiotic should be prescribed, he will customarily ask the patient if he is allergic to any such medication. If the patient is unaware of an allergy, begins to take the prescribed medication, and has an unexpected allergic reaction, that is not malpractice. The doctor examined the patient carefully, arrived at a correct diagnosis, and prescribed a course of treatment that, under normal circumstances, would have been correct. The patient didn't know about the allergy; neither did the physician. Certainly, if this physician was able to relive that situation, he would prescribe a different antibiotic. If it is an honest misjudgment, there is no legal liability.

But this is not what the malpractice crisis is all about. In most of the cases we see the malpractice is so blatant that it is sometimes difficult to comprehend or believe. It screams out for redress.

The single biggest cause of malpractice—and malpractice lawsuits—is a physician's simply not showing up. An emergency call reaches them at home late at night, or at a social engagement, and they decide without ever seeing the patient that the problem is nothing to worry about. Whether it's a child with a fever or an expectant mother beginning to have contractions, the negligent doctor decides on the basis of a phone call that it's not critical for him to see the patient. There is nothing to warrant getting out of bed or interrupting an evening at the theater.

Except that there is no way of telling—without actually examining the patient—whether the fever is caused by a virus that will pass in a day or by something more serious. There's no way of knowing whether fetal distress is going to occur in the labor room, while the doctor is watching the second act of a play.

A second common medical failure—neglecting to take a complete medical history—accounts for a significant additional amount of malpractice. Approximately 80 percent of all accurate diagnoses are based on information that is part of the patient's medical history. Medical texts make this argument repeatedly, as in *Grinker's Neurology:* "A complete history is often the most important single item in establishing a diagnosis and instituting therapy; a fragmentary and inaccurate account may lead to confusion and actually delay the proper management of the problem at hand."

The taking of histories, however, is one of the most neglected areas in the practice of medicine, for one reason: The process takes time and patience. It requires the physician to ask questions, to learn about the patient's past and present habits, family, trips abroad, other related ailments. Often, the patient is the worst judge of what is wrong and presents volumes of irrelevant information. It is up to the physician to ask the right questions, to probe until he or she finds the clues that will lead to the correct diagnosis.

The cause of a patient's stomach ailment, for example, might be a mystery. The patient may describe to the doctor his eating habits and other information, but the doctor will not come to the correct conclusion until he learns that, a year ago, the patient made a trip to Mexico, where he contracted dysentery. The patient thought it had passed, but had never been properly treated. That key piece of information alerts the physician to the possibility that the parasites that caused the dysentery had never been destroyed and had caused a recurrence of the symptoms. But he would never have considered that diagnosis if he had not taken the time to find out about the patient's travels of a year earlier.

In much the same way, physical examinations are often given short shrift for no reason other than the physician's laziness and unfounded conviction that he knows what he's doing and doesn't need to go through all the basics. But doctors who jump to conclusions based on their "experience," without taking the time to conduct a proper top-to-bottom examination of each patient, are kidding themselves and asking for trouble. Medical diagnosis is based on a methodical, scientific approach, not guesswork. Ignoring this basic of good medicine places the patient at significant risk.

Keeping in mind that these three major medical faults are common to most cases of malpractice, we have found that there are also certain medical specialties with a particularly high incidence of negligence—areas in which doctors and patients clearly have to exercise greater caution.

Without a doubt, the most malpractice occurs in obstetrics. The single biggest problem is obstetricians who don't show up in the labor room when the mother goes into labor. While the doctor is home in bed or otherwise occupied, trouble develops with the fetus and there is no one there to do anything about it.

Ann Richards and her husband Larry, a factory worker in a midwestern city, were expecting their first child. They did what most people do in this situation: They asked their family doctor and some neighbors who had just had a baby for recommendations of obstetricians.

They settled on Dr. Alex Strawski, who was affiliated with the hospital near the Richards's home. Ann saw him throughout her pregnancy, which proceeded normally, and was perfectly content as her new child grew within her.

When the time came, a little before midnight, Ann woke Larry, they dressed quickly, grabbed her already packed overnight bag, and rushed to the hospital. Right after being admitted, the general-practice resident on duty examined Ann, and she asked him to call Dr. Strawski to let him know of her condition so that he could come to the hospital. She had got comfortable with Dr. Strawski over the past months and wanted to be sure that he was the one who delivered her baby.

When the resident telephoned Dr. Strawski, he declined to come to the hospital. It was the middle of the night, the young resident had awakened him from a sound sleep, and Dr. Strawski told him to monitor the labor and call him again when it was time to deliver the baby. The resident hooked Ann up to an electronic fetal monitor, which is a normal precaution. This device monitors the fetus's heart rate while the mother is in labor.

During the night, trouble began. There was a cephalo pelvic disproportion—the baby's head was too large to move through the mother's pelvis. The monitor showed fetal distress; the baby was asphyxiating. A cesarean section would have to be performed immediately.

The resident, unqualified to perform the surgery himself, called Dr. Strawski, again awakening him. Dr. Strawski hung up the phone and went back to bed. The resident was desperate. It was 2:00 A.M.; there was no one on duty who could help. He called Dr. Strawski again. Again, he was ignored. He called a total of five times during the night, but couldn't rouse the doctor sufficiently to get him to visit his patient in the hospital, where her baby was suffocating. A shortage of oxygen was causing more and more damage to the brain of the fetus with each hour that passed.

Dr. Strawski finally arrived some time after 8:00 A.M., and delivered the baby. It was irreparably brain-damaged and quadriplegic. In investigating this case, we questioned a number of the obstetric nurses who work at this hospital. Apparently Dr. Strawski never likes to be disturbed during the night. He does this all the time, particularly when his patients are poor and he has doubts about whether his bill will be paid. Usually he and his patients are fortunate—nothing goes wrong.

Ninety-five percent of all deliveries are easy. Anyone can do them. The friend who referred Ann and Larry Richards to Dr. Strawski was one of those 95 percent. But in approximately 5 percent of the cases, problems develop. If the physician is not there to recognize trouble when it occurs, the result can be disastrous.

How does this happen? How can a physician be so negligent? Well, no one likes waiting around a labor room for hours, with little likelihood of anything happening. It's much easier to stay home or go about your business, and tell the nurse on duty to call when the mother is ready to give birth. This is especially true if it's late at night, as it was in Ann Richards's case. That strategy, however, in addition to requiring the doctor to show up when he actually has to, requires a nurse able to recognize the early signs of fetal distress.

What happens if it's a busy hospital? What happens if it's short staffed? Or if a lot of mothers happen to go into labor at the same time? What if the nurse who is supposed to be monitoring the labor of one patient is called into the delivery room to assist another who is further along?

What often happens is that the hospital calls in floaters—nurses from another department—or the medical equivalent of "temps," who may or may not know how to read a fetal monitor.

The fetal monitor is a device that is wrapped around the abdomen of the mother, counts the heart rate of the fetus, and prints it out on a tape that looks much like an electrocardiogram (EKG). The normal heartrate of a fetus in labor is between 120 and 160 beats per minute. If it drops below 120 and stays there, it means the baby is not getting enough oxygen—it's asphyxiating and has to be delivered by cesarean immediately. If the heart rate is too fast, it is a sign that the heart is not functioning efficiently, also probably because of a decreased flow of oxygen.

It takes a trained individual to monitor this activity. Normally the fetal heart rate decreases during contractions. If it slows immediately following a contraction, the pelvis could be compressing the umbilical cord or the placenta could be separating from the uterus, cutting off or reducing the oxygen supplied to the baby. In such cases the child must be delivered immediately. But that observation requires a trained eye in the labor room, paying careful attention to the monitor. And it requires a physician on the scene to deal with the situation. If he's an hour away at home or on the golf course, he could be too late. Or if, like Dr. Strawski, he simply refuses to get out of bed, he will definitely be too late, and the life of an infant—of an entire family, really—will be devastated.

In another obstetric case, so much negligence and incompetence occurred that it is difficult to understand how the doctors can live with themselves. Judy Heimann had been in labor for a long time and her obstetrician, Dr. Roger Barber, was getting impatient. He ordered Pitocin, a drug which induces contractions. She was also in considerable pain, although it's impossible to know now whether her discomfort was greater than usual for the childbirth process, so Dr. Barber ordered heavy narcotics to dull her senses. Narcotics are rarely used on expectant mothers because whatever drugs are given to the mother go right through the bloodstream to the fetus. Depressants administered to a mother in labor will also depress the unborn child. And the dosage necessary to anesthetize a mother is huge when applied to an infant.

In those unusual cases in which narcotics are necessary, they can be used if other drugs are administered at the same time to counteract their effect on the fetus. But Judy Heimann never received this second type of drug. When we questioned the anesthesiologist who was present during the delivery, he had an interesting response. He didn't know what she had been given, he said, because he had never looked at her medical chart.

But that's not the worst of it. Dr. Barber had ordered Pitocin to induce contractions. That's very common under certain circumstances, but Ms. Heimann's delivery was a breech. In a normal delivery, the child's head comes out first. In a breech, the fetus is positioned with the buttocks coming out first. There is a serious danger that the umbilical cord will be compressed or the head—normally the largest part of the fetus—will get stuck. A cesarean section should be performed immediately in most cases to prevent the child from being destroyed.

Certainly such a patient should never be given Pitocin. Because of the position of the fetus, the contractions can potentially cause the uterus to contract and press down on the cord, cutting off the baby's oxygen supply. And that's what happened here. With each contraction that the Pitocin caused, the fetus was being choked. When it was born, the child was barely breathing.

The health of newborn babies is graded according to Apgar ratings, a scale that measures heart rate, respiration, body tone, and other factors. The scale goes from 0 to 10, with a perfect baby rated 10. When this child was born, he was given an Apgar of 5. After five minutes, he was rated a 6, a marginal improvement but still a critical situation.

A half-hour prior to the delivery, recognizing that he had a problem, Dr. Barber had called for a pediatrician to treat the child after birth. By the time of delivery, the pediatrician had not yet arrived. The baby Dr. Barber delivered was barely breathing, barely alive. What emergency measures did Dr. Barber take next? He sent the infant to the nursery.

Here was an infant barely breathing, in obvious and imminent risk of brain damage, sent to the nursery to lie in a crib and wait for the pediatrician. Not that the pediatrician's presence, when he arrived an hour and a half later, made any difference. This doctor examined the child but refused to order oxygen. He said the child was cold. The child was cold because he had aspirated (suffered from a lack of oxygen). He wasn't breathing, and this physician would not give him oxygen. Eventually, someone realized—much too late—that the child was brain-damaged.

The penalties against these doctors? The anesthesiologist who administered narcotics without reading the patient's chart? The obstetrician who botched the delivery, then sent a baby who wasn't breathing to the nursery? The pediatrician who showed up 90 minutes late and refused to give that baby oxygen? No penalty whatsoever.

What resulted was a civil lawsuit that, as of this writing, is still pending. No sanctions have been imposed against these physicians, by the hospital or by the state in which they practice. Nothing has been done to prevent them from treating more unsuspecting patients.

Negligence by physicians in obstetrics is far more widespread than most people realize and is responsible for far more damage than the medical profession will acknowledge. In fact, many types of birth defects that society accepts as inevitable are the direct result of malpractice and are totally avoidable.

A 1977 study of cerebral palsy patients entitled "Is Cerebral Palsy a Preventable Disease?" found that 38 percent of these patients had received inadequate and inappropriate obstetric or neonatal care. Cerebral palsy, a condition caused by injury to the brain, can result from a number of causes, some of which are inevitable. But many causes are due to hypoxia—a substantial shortage of oxygen to the brain—which is often the result of medical negligence.

Autism, a disease of the brain which leads to an inability to speak and communicate, can be caused by the same type of malpractice. Although it is often the result of other problems, and usually considered to be a psychological phenomenon, autism can also sometimes be attributed to hypoxia, which in many cases can be prevented.

Another very common condition, Erb's Palsy, is virtually always the result of malpractice. Erb's Palsy is a deformity of the arm, shoulder, and hand area that makes the arm appear somewhat twisted and shriveled, so that the hand hangs limply and is pointed backward. It has afflicted countless patients who, for the most part, lose the effective use of their arm for life. One of its most notable victims was Kaiser Wilhelm II, who led Germany into

World War I, always photographed holding a glove on his hand in an effort to make his arm seem longer.

Erb's Palsy occurs when the brachial plexus nerves in the neck and shoulder area are damaged during delivery. There is no other logical way for it to happen and, in fact, it is almost always due to the obstetrician's negligence. Sometimes the position of the baby's head is slightly askew when it starts coming out, tilted or leaning against one shoulder or the other. If the shoulder is too large to make it through the pelvis easily, the delivery is a little more difficult. The proper course is a Woods Maneuver, in which the obstetrician pushes the baby back into the mother and tries to reposition him. But this takes time and some doctors are impatient, so they take the baby's head and pull, ripping the nerves that control the function of the arm and leaving the child deformed for life.

This unfortunate habit of a doctor's not showing up personally to examine and attend to the patient is a flaw common to many practitioners of obstetrics and pediatrics. Just as obstetricians are often disturbed at inopportune times by expectant mothers going into labor, pediatricians get phone calls at all hours from anxious parents. That's nothing extraordinary. It's part of the job, and physicians in these specialties should be prepared for it and willing to accept the responsibility of being on call.

Infants are prone to infection. In the first days after birth, the area where the umbilical cord was cut is very sensitive. With diapers being frequently soiled, it is nearly impossible to keep this area completely clean. Pediatricians and parents should be alert to this possibility because, if infections occur and go untreated, they can become septic and cause severe problems. For example, a mother who happened to be a nurse brought her eleven-day-old baby to the hospital one night shortly after midnight. The baby had a high fever and his diapers were constantly wet. The norm in such a case is to assume the existence of an infection, do bacterial cultures as soon as possible—within forty-five minutes—and start administering antibiotics intravenously.

An hour passed and nothing was done. No culture. No antibiotics. The attending physician never came into the room to examine the baby. The child convulsed. Still, nothing was done. Convulsions continued.

Infections and fevers in small children often lead to seizures, as happened in this instance. Repeated seizures—known as status epilepticus—that go on for hours may cause hypoxia, or in some cases the seizures may be caused by hypoxia. They are extremely dangerous because of the risk of brain damage, and they must be stopped by any means necessary, even if medication is required to put the patient to sleep.

The staff at this hospital watched the baby convulsing for hours—entering three pages of copious notes about the convulsions in his chart—but no doctor examined the child. In the hours it took before there was action to stop this infant's seizures and treat the infection, he suffered severe brain damage. If he had been examined immediately and treated promptly, none of this damage would have occurred.

Another area of medicine in which we have seen a great deal of malpractice is the diagnosis and treatment of cancer. Errors in clinical diagnosis are made in as many as 40 percent of the cases in which cancer patients ultimately die, and mistakes are often made in treating even the most common forms of cancer—the ones about which physicians should be the most informed.

Because of the devastating nature of this disease, most of its victims expect the worst, but actually many forms of cancer are treatable if discovered at a sufficiently early stage. Some forms of malignant cancer—of the brain or pancreas, for example—are generally incurable. But breast cancer, colon cancer, and uterine cancer have high cure rates—perhaps 70 percent to 80 percent if identified in time.

What is most unfortunate are those cases in which a curable form of cancer is not diagnosed or treated until it has reached an advanced stage. By then it has grown and spread to the point where the patient has little chance of survival. Sometimes this delay occurs because the patient doesn't recognize the symptoms, doesn't report them to a doctor, doesn't go for regular checkups.

Time passes until he or she experiences pain, bleeding, or other symptoms that are impossible to ignore. By the time the cancer is diagnosed, it is too late.

It's not always the patient's fault, though. Many patients undergo examinations during which the physicians have an opportunity to recognize a cancer in its early stage. But either through negligence or incompetence, they fail to note what could be a serious problem. In "What are the chances when malignancy leads to a malpractice suit?," in fact, an insurance company study of lawsuits involving allegations of malpractice in the treatment of cancer by authors Michael Mittleman and Charles Scholhamer, revealed that 75 percent of the cases involved an allegation of delay in diagnosis. Nineteen percent involved an allegation of improper treatment, and 6 percent involved a failure to provide adequate information to the patient.

These are the kind of mistakes physicians are specifically taught to guard against. *Cecil's Textbook of Medicine,* for example, notes that:

> Too often, previous examinations are accepted in lieu of a fresh, independent look, to the patient's detriment. A detailed chronological development of all the symptomatology must be undertaken with care, and the patient's observations must not be dismissed because they do not happen to fit the pattern of a disease process the physician is entertaining. What a patient says is to be believed and to be understood to the best of the physician's ability. Thus, if a woman tells her physician that she has noted a breast lump, but he is not impressed because of extensive multiple lumps of cystic mastitis, nevertheless, if she has noted one lump above all others, the observation must be believed and acted upon. Too often, the physician attempts to reassure prematurely with a pat on the hand and thereby, in effect, to impose his wisdom on the patient.

In the most troubling cases we've seen—"textbook" cases, it seems—doctors performed examinations, actually recognized the existence of tumors, and did nothing about them. They apparently thought it was not important to send the patients for further tests. When a delay in diagnosis or treatment of a treatable cancer occurs because of physician failure to conduct a proper examination or to recognize the seriousness of what the examination reveals, the doctor's actions could be considered the equivalent of sentencing the patient to death.

Sheila Howard's family became our clients in 1988 after her death from breast cancer, a death they believed could have been avoided. Ms. Howard, a forty-two-year-old executive, noticed during a self-examination that she had a small lump in her breast. Concerned, she immediately scheduled an appointment for an examination with her physician, Dr. Ralph Hawkins.

He too felt a lump in her breast, and actually noted his finding on her chart. The standard course of treatment is to have a mammogram done. After reviewing the results of the mammogram, the prudent course is to refer the patient for a biopsy. Even if the mammogram comes back negative, when the physician feels the presence of a lump, he should have it biopsied to be certain it isn't malignant.

Dr. Hawkins didn't recommend a mammogram for Ms. Howard. Nor did he suggest that a biopsy might be in order. He told his patient not to be concerned, that it was probably nothing, and to make another appointment to see him nine months later. Sheila Howard trusted her doctor. He must know what he's doing. In fact, she was relieved that he thought she had nothing to worry about.

Nine months later, her body was riddled with cancer. She died soon afterward.

Breast cancer is something about which even laypeople have become knowledgeable in recent years. Numerous magazine and newspaper articles have been written, describing the risk of delay and the need for early detection. Dr. Hawkins obviously had not read any of those magazines. He sent his patient home to wait for nine months for her cancer to kill her.

On behalf of the Howard family, we brought a lawsuit for malpractice against Dr. Hawkins. When the facts came to light—it was no mystery; all the relevant information was contained in the patient's medical records—the doctor's insurance company agreed to pay a $1.5 million settlement. What happened to Dr. Hawkins? Nothing. He continued practicing medicine. His patients never learned anything about this incident.

We see this type of mistreatment and delay almost every day and not only with breast cancer cases. The most common cause of anemia, or "tired blood," in patients aged forty to sixty years old is cancer of the colon. This form of cancer is also associated with rectal bleeding. The proper course of treatment when a person in this age group complains of these symptoms is to determine whether cancer is present by doing a colonoscopy—inserting a scope into the rectum up through the interior of the colon—or a barium enema, which causes defects in the colon to become visible in X-rays. When detected in its early stages, the cancerous polyp or tumor can be removed from the colon and the cure rate is approximately 80 percent.

What we have seen, however, are cases where doctors examine patients, find them to be anemic, and rather than check for the presence of cancer, they give them a prescription for iron pills and send them on their way. Or, as we saw in the case of Rita Dole, they notice rectal bleeding, attribute it to hemorrhoids, and send the patient home with suppositories, without a thorough examination of the colon.

Colon cancer is rated according to the Duke's classification—A, B, C, or D, with D as worst. By the time a cancer reaches the D stage, it has broken through the wall of the colon and spread to the liver or other organs. However, when patients notice a problem and seek medical advice while the cancer is at one of the earlier stages—A or B—the physician should not send them away with iron pills and some hemorrhoid cream.

Another form of cancer—uterine cancer—is usually seen in postmenopausal women. In fact, when a patient at this stage of life experiences a discharge of blood, the physician is supposed to assume it is cancer until tests prove otherwise. The proper course is to perform a dilatation and curettage, or scraping, and to have the results analyzed to determine whether cancerous cells are present. If it is found early, and surgery is performed to remove the patient's uterus, the survival rate is approximately 80 percent.

Doing tests, putting a patient in the hospital, do not require all that much effort. Nevertheless, we've seen cases of uterine cancer where doctors apparently decided it was too much effort. Rather than do the work necessary to rule out cancer, they prescribed a variety of creams and lotions, sent their patients home, and ignored the cancer.

Another form of cancer with which most Americans are all too familiar, and which has afflicted millions of people, is lung cancer. In recent years many internists, and some general practitioners, have had chest X-ray machinery installed in their offices. Sometimes, when patients are referred elsewhere for tests, they put it off and simply don't go. Having these machines in the office makes doing the X-ray more convenient for both doctor and patient.

There's only one problem. A lot of the doctors doing chest X-rays don't know how to read and accurately evaluate the results. Presumably, they are either too arrogant or too cost-conscious to have the X-rays reviewed by a trained radiologist.

Lung cancer can be identified on a chest X-ray for up to two and a half years before it reaches the stage where it is inoperable. If caught early, it also has a reasonable cure rate. Internists and general practitioners, with no training in radiology, should not be reading X-rays without consulting radiologists, and making judgments on whether or not they reveal the presence of cancer. All too often they get it wrong. The patient waits, years go by, and the patient dies.

Another significant area in which malpractice occurs is in surgery. This is a specialty, however, in which the patients—as well as the doctors—can play a meaningful role in avoiding injuries due to negligence.

According to Jane Brody's January 1976, report in the *New York Times,* "the evidence is that even the safest surgery is never without some risk to the patient's life and that the American surgical profession, which is probably the best trained in the world, contains a number of unethical, incompetent and careless practitioners." We don't intend this information to discourage patients who are in need of surgery for serious medical reasons. However, medical need is not the most common reason for undergoing surgery.

Approximately 80 percent of the 18 million Americans who have surgery every year undergo elective procedures. In other words, the surgery was not immediately required and could have been avoided, at least temporarily. In fact, it is likely that between one-third and two-thirds of certain types of elective surgery are contrary to the patient's interests.

One out of 200 patients die as a result of elective surgery, according to a study by the American College of Surgeons and the American Surgical Association, and nearly half of nonfatal complications and nearly one-third of deaths that result from elective surgery are preventable. That's 24,000 avoidable deaths and 36,000 avoidable injuries from elective surgeries in America each year. Seventy-eight percent of these preventable deaths and injuries are due to surgeon errors.

According to the *New York Times* report of the study, many of these deaths

> are the direct result of careless errors made by doctors or others involved in the patient's care. . . . Even a very small risk can add up to a substantial number of deaths and other mishaps. For example, tonsillectomy is one of the safest operations, with only 2 in 10,000 patients dying as a result of such an operation. But since 724,000 tonsillectomies are done in a year, nearly 150 patients—mostly children—die annually as a result. Some experts maintain that 70 percent of these operations are of little or no value to the patient. It could mean, if this estimate is correct, that the lives of perhaps 100 people are lost unnecessarily each year because they are subjected to needless tonsillectomies.

Unnecessary surgery falls into two categories: nonessential surgery patients elect to have done—plastic surgery, for instance;

and surgery that a doctor recommends, purportedly for medical reasons, that proves to have been uncalled for. In 1976, the House Subcommittee on Oversight and Investigations of the Committee on Interstate and Foreign Commerce reported on the results of a study conducted by Dr. Eugene G. McCarthy and Geraldine W. Widmer of the Cornell University Medical College. Reports by the congressional committee indicate that, when patients seek second opinions, approximately 20 percent of consulting physicians discourage them from having the surgery originally recommended. According to this research, 2.4 million unnecessary operations are performed in America each year, and nearly 12,000 lives are lost as a result.

Sophie Gross, a seventy-one-year-old woman with osteoporosis, went to her doctor complaining of pain in her legs when she walked. She and her husband, a former city employee, were members of a health maintenance organization (HMO) through his union retirement plan. They were assigned by the health plan to a vascular surgeon, Dr. Emil Rani, who diagnosed Ms. Gross as having obstructions to the blood flow in her legs. Surgery would be needed to clear them.

Prior to the surgery, she was admitted to the hospital, where an angiogram (the insertion of a catheter that allows doctors to examine the inside of a blood vessel) was performed to determine the exact location of the blockages. After the test, ice and pressure had to be applied by her physicians to stop what was an unusually excessive amount of bleeding from the groin area. She was released from the hospital that day.

When Dr. Rani saw Sophie Gross several days later, he told her he was surprised at the bleeding and the bruising that had developed in the area, and that she should never have an angiogram performed in that hospital again. But he then admitted her to the same hospital to have the surgery performed to remove the blood clots.

When she woke up the day after her surgery, Ms. Gross could not feel or move her legs. In the hours that followed, the attending physicians and nurses noted in her medical records a lack of movement of her lower extremities. At the first sign of this paralysis, her doctors should have considered the possibility that there was a blood clot causing pressure on her spinal cord. That would have been the most logical explanation. But it was not until almost a full day had passed that any tests were performed. When the tests finally were done, the myelogram (a picture of the spinal cord) revealed that a blood clot was indeed present. Surgery would be needed, it was decided, but this particular hospital lacked the facilities to perform it.

Remember, this hospital was part of an HMO. One of the ways in which HMOs save money is by requiring patients to use, whenever possible, only physicians and hospitals that are part of their network. In emergency cases, however, the health of the patient is supposed to take precedence over dollars and cents. But rather than referring Ms. Gross to a nearby hospital with more adequate surgical facilities, her physicians—who had already left her lying in bed paralyzed for a full twenty-four hours—put her in an ambulance and transferred her to a hospital that participated in that HMO. It took another four hours for her to be relocated.

At the second hospital, a magnetic resonance imaging (MRI) was performed in addition to a CAT scan. The neurosurgeons located the blood clot, which had affected the nerves that control the lower part of the body. If they had got to Gross sooner, they would have performed surgery to remove that clot and she would have had a good chance of recovering the use of her legs. But with all the time that had passed, they believed that too much damage had been done and that, given the patient's age, surgery would be counterproductive. She would be paralyzed, they said, for the rest of her life.

Ms. Gross was then transferred back to the original hospital, where the horrors continued. She developed bedsores on her legs, which can be a sign of only one thing: neglect. It is a simple matter to prevent bedsores in a paralyzed patient; it requires competent nursing care, keeping the patient clean and applying powder occasionally. There is certainly no excuse for a hospital allowing these bedsores to develop. But that is exactly what happened. The bedsores became infected, and on one leg the infection became severe. Eventually, almost the entire left leg had to be amputated.

Since then, Ms. Gross has remained in the hospital, where she is at this time. During the course of her hospitalization, she contracted pneumonia and sustained a collapsed lung. She is on a respirator and communicates with her husband, who is always at her side, mostly through short, handwritten notes.

Malpractice? No question about it. The more than twenty-four-hour delay in noticing that the patient couldn't move her legs and the more prolonged delay in properly diagnosing the blood clot compressing her spinal cord were the clear cause of Sophie Gross's ensuing paralysis. Allowing bedsores to develop and become infected is obvious negligence, the cause of her losing her leg.

The more significant point, however, is that the original surgery—to deal with the pain Ms. Gross experienced when walking—was not necessary. It need never have been performed at all. A seventy-one-year-old woman with vascular compromise can have some trouble walking. While she complained of some difficulty, this patient was able to walk up to ten blocks prior to her surgery. Other courses of treatment, including physical therapy, should certainly have been tried before surgery. Surgery on a woman of her age carries with it significant risks under the best circumstances, and in this case it was totally uncalled for. Most competent physicians would agree that, in the face of those risks, advising the patient to get used to living with some discomfort is by far the more prudent option.

The Sophie Gross case involved a patient following the advice of her physician. She thought the surgery and the treatment she received were medically necessary. Another form of unnecessary surgery involves the type of elective surgery that a patient chooses to have, usually plastic or cosmetic surgery. For the most part, cosmetic surgery is performed on parts of the body that function normally, in an effort to improve the patient's appearance. In some cases, such as in burn victims who undergo skin grafts or cancer patients who have been through a mastectomy and wish to have reconstructive surgery, this type of surgery is associated with a medical condition. In many other cases, the patient simply wants to look better. In either of these situations, there are significant risks.

With one of every 200 elective surgery patients—24,000 people a year—dying unnecessarily, anyone who is a candidate for elective surgery—whose health is not at stake—should think very carefully before having such a procedure.

Perhaps the most celebrated cases of cosmetic surgery going awry involve patients who have had silicon breast implants. There has been evidence for years that these implants pose health risks, with lawsuits against implant manufacturers dating back more than a decade. In *The American Law of Medical Malpractice,* a legal text we published in 1982, we warned that breast enlargement could cause physical problems and that "complications have been reported" in patients who have had silicone breast implants.

We reported at that time on a 1980 case in which a woman had sued both her plastic surgeon and an implant manufacturer:

> A mammary augmentation was performed by the defendant plastic surgeon on the plaintiff by means of inserting artificial breast implants filled with a soft silicon gel. Postoperatively, the patient had swelling, soreness and inflammation of her breasts, and the patient was re-hospitalized to remove the implant and drain a hematoma and to insert a new implant. The patient however, continued to have pain and inflammation, and her condition was ultimately diagnosed as siliconomas, which were nodules caused by the accumulation of migrating silicon gel. The patient was required to undergo over twenty surgical operations to remove the siliconomas, as they continued to appear. The plaintiff settled her suit with the manufacturer of the breast implants and went to trial against the surgeon. . . .

In this case, the jury ruled in favor of the plastic surgeon. This was 1980, and at the time there was no evidence that he had departed from the normal standard of care. Implants were commonly performed by many doctors, and the jury did not believe that the physician had reason to know these complications would develop.

There is no way of proving what knowledge that particular plastic surgeon had or didn't have. But according to an investigation by the *Wall Street Journal* (March 12, 1992), evidence had been presented to the plastic surgery community of complications associated with silicon implants as early as 1976:

> While the silicon-implant debate has focused on whether manufacturers hid suspected risks from the public, there is evidence that over the past two decades, plastic surgeons themselves saw and ignored red flags in this lucrative branch of their specialty. Critics say many plastic surgeons failed to alert women to possible health risks reported by several sources, including professional journals, manufacturers and some of their own patients.

After one manufacturer received back from surgeons 140 ruptured implants for replacement during a thirteen-month period, the president of the company wrote to his clients that "doctors and patients should expect that some patients will exhibit some adverse response to silicone implants." The *Wall Street Journal* reported anecdotal evidence in medical journals going back to 1979, "describing how one patient suffered fevers, sweats, swollen joints and enlarged kidneys within days of getting silicone-gel implants." In 1986, there were reports "documenting cases of three silicone-implant patients who had joint pain, including one who lost partial use of an arm."

All of these warnings were rejected by plastic surgeons, who are continuing to wage a multimillion-dollar lobbying effort to return implants to general use. At this time, the FDA is allowing their implantation only in such limited cases as those of women who wish to have reconstructive surgery following mastectomies.

All of the thousands of women who have had serious health problems as a result of silicone implants "elected" to have this surgery performed on them. There are virtually no circumstances under which these implants are required to improve health. They made their decisions on the false assumption—sometimes encouraged by their surgeons—that there are few if any risks associated with this procedure. The silicone implant situation is indeed a horror story. Not all elective surgery turns out the same way. But it illustrates the need for patients to understand the significant risks associated with surgery, and to avoid surgery when the benefits are minimal.

Another medical practitioner most people come into contact with at some point in their lives is the orthopedic surgeon—the physician whose specialty involves the diagnosis and treatment of broken bones, dislocated joints, pulled muscles, torn ligaments, and all the injuries and diseases that affect the structure of the human body. We also see a lot of orthopedic surgeons in medical malpractice cases.

Since most people come in contact with an orthopedic surgeon when they injure themselves, they usually get to them via the hospital emergency room. When a patient meets up with an incompetent orthopedic surgeon in the midst of a busy emergency room, it can be a very risky combination indeed.

Sean O'Connor's parents had always worried about his riding a dirt bike, and they warned him constantly to be careful. The seventeen-year-old understood their concern and was usually cautious, wearing a helmet and staying fairly close to home.

But one day Sean was riding around his family's farm—fairly slowly, as a matter of fact—when the bike hit a patch of mud and he skidded. As the bike went down, Sean reached out his arm to break his fall and the arm was injured.

His mother rushed him to the local emergency room, where Dr. Duc Kwan examined him and ordered X-rays, which confirmed his diagnosis of a fractured wrist. Dr. Kwan put a cast on the injured area and, just as a precaution, admitted Sean to the hospital for observation.

A few hours later, the patient was moaning in pain, calling the nurses for help and asking them to provide some relief. Dr. Kwan examined him again, and found that Sean's hand was becoming cold and discolored. Under these circumstances, most physicians would probably conclude that the cast was too tight, cutting off the flow of blood to the hand. The proper course would be to remove the cast and reset the arm so the cast holds the injured bone in place but, at the same time, allows the blood to circulate normally.

Dr. Kwan didn't do those things. Instead, he prescribed codeine for the pain and ordered the staff to elevate Sean's hand from an IV pole. Sean remained in the hospital for five days. During that time, he was given codeine regularly and, not surprisingly, his hand and wrist felt better.

When Dr. Kwan sent him home, he told Sean and his mother that the swelling and discoloration of the hand were to be expected and that it would return to normal within a few days. He explained to them the importance of keeping Sean's hand elevated while he was at home. He told them to drill a hole in his bedroom ceiling and screw a hook into it, from which to hang a device that would keep the arm raised. He continued the prescription for codeine, which the patient was to take as needed. Sean was happy to be going home.

Sean was released from the hospital on a Friday. During the weekend, despite the codeine and despite hanging his hand from the hook as Dr. Kwan had recommended, Sean was in agony. First thing Monday morning, Mrs. O'Connor took Sean back to the doctor, who examined Sean's discolored hand.

When Dr. Kwan finally removed the cast, he should have realized what would have been obvious days earlier to any competent physician: the entire hand and wrist area were putrified. The too-tight cast had cut off the blood supply for an extended period of time, and in simple terms, part of the patient's arm had simply died. But this was not sufficient to alert Dr. Kwan. He referred Sean for whirlpool treatments.

If this had not been done negligently, it would have been sadistic. Sean went for the whirlpool and watched as pieces of his dead arm fell off in the water. What did Dr. Kwan do? He dressed the arm in a loose bandage and recommended another whirlpool treatment in a few days. Sean came back, went into the whirlpool again, and more of the rotted tissue peeled off. Finally, after seeking the advice of other physicians who warned him of the risk of spreading infection, Sean had almost his entire arm amputated.

When this incident took place, Dr. Kwan was the hospital's chief of surgery. Although we sued on Sean's behalf and obtained a substantial settlement, Dr. Kwan remains in that position today.

Unfortunately, this type of orthopedic mistreatment—horrifying as it is—is not a remote occurrence. Misdiagnoses often result from a misreading of X-rays. The improper application of casts, as happened to Sean O'Connor, and the failure to correct them when circulatory problems become evident, is a major cause of patient injury and one of the significant bases of malpractice lawsuits.

In an Arkansas case, a patient was admitted to the hospital and had a cast applied to correct a fracture of two bones in his leg. After three days in the hospital the patient began to complain that he couldn't move his toes. His foot appeared to be swollen. Throughout the night, he complained, and a notation was made in his chart that his toes were cool and discolored. The attending physician, apparently not wanting to come to the hospital at that hour to examine his patient, directed a nurse to cut a hole in the cast and move it slightly with her hands. This relieved the patient's pain for a while, but the following day he again complained of pain, now growing more severe. Again by telephone, the physician ordered the cast cut and moved slightly, which alleviated the pain temporarily.

Two days after the patient began experiencing pain, discoloration, and an inability to move his toes, his physician finally examined him in the hospital. He noted continued discoloration and lack of movement, but did nothing. After another day passed he ordered the patient transferred to a different hospital for additional treatment.

Of course, the cast had been too tight and cutting holes in it didn't do any good. The doctor who had set the leg apparently didn't want to be bothered removing the cast and applying a new one. So when an orthopedic surgeon at the second hospital examined this patient, he found that the foot had been destroyed. He was forced to remove the entire lower portion of the patient's leg.

The treatment—or mistreatment—of broken bones and other orthopedic injuries is obviously just one of the things patients have to worry about in the hectic, often disorganized atmosphere of the emergency room. With doctors and nurses rushing from patient to patient in an often overcrowded, understaffed facility, errors in diagnosis occur with great regularity, in a host of medical specialties.

When a patient of a certain age—midforties to midfifties or above—complains of chest or abdominal pains, the standard course of treatment is to assume he or she has had a myocardial infarction, or heart attack, until tests prove otherwise. But often the hospital staff either forgets or doesn't have time to perform an EKG—or if they do perform it, they fail to read it accurately. Or they simply don't bother doing a thorough examination of the patient.

Jack Hooper worked in midtown Manhattan, his office located within minutes of some of the finest medical centers in the world. When he began feeling a tightness in his chest one afternoon, he walked down the stairs from his third-floor office and along the few blocks to one of these hospitals. He went through the emergency room and, after what passed for an examination, he was sent back to the office with a clean bill of health and a note explaining his brief absence. Mr. Hooper returned to his office, walked over to his boss to explain where he'd been, and collapsed dead in the man's arms.

The hospital argued that something must have happened to Mr. Hooper after he left the hospital, that it couldn't be responsible for his death. But the autopsy revealed that Mr. Hooper's legs were badly swollen. This type of swelling, known as edema, takes many hours to develop. Therefore, it could not have occurred in the short time after he left the hospital and it could clearly not have occurred after death. It must have been present when he was in the emergency room. Swollen legs are a symptom of congestive heart failure. The condition that caused his fatal heart attack had to have existed at the time the emergency room staff conducted its examination—if it had conducted an examination.

The swollen legs should have been a tip-off for the correct diagnosis. Had the doctors seen Mr. Hooper's legs, they never would have allowed him to leave the hospital. But obviously, in performing their "examination," they didn't ask the patient to remove his pants.

There is another area in which physicians often fail to take sufficient care of their patients—in the prescription of various drugs. According to a *New York Times* report dated January 28, 1976, it is likely that 30,000 Americans die each year as a result of drugs misprescribed by doctors. And 300,000 more probably suffer serious, sometimes long-term side effects, from internal bleeding to blindness. The *Times* article noted that a study by the Boston Collaborative Drug Surveillance Program estimated that 300,000 people annually are *hospitalized* as a result of bad reactions to drugs, making this one of the leading causes of hospitalization in America. This study, directed by a physician from Boston University Medical Center, also found that one in every eighteen prescriptions written in a hospital results in a negative reaction. Of those reactions, 10 percent have serious consequences and 1.2 percent are fatal. The same *New York Times* article states: "Other studies have suggested there may be as many as 160,000 deaths a year due to drug reactions. Such studies are hotly disputed by the drug industry."

The misprescription of drugs can occur when patients seek treatment for virtually any illness. There are about 12,000 different drugs on the market. They are prescribed by neurologists, obstetricians, internists, and physicians in other specialties as well. Despite the obvious differences among all these specialties, and despite the fact that no drug is completely safe, there is no prohibition against any physician prescribing any drug for any use— regardless of whether he or she is sufficiently familiar with its benefits, risks, and possible side effects.

According to the *Times* article, even officials of the AMA have admitted that "a problem of preventable adverse drug reactions exists. . . . The literature abounds with references to the prescription of the wrong drug or dose, to unforeseen drug reactions, or simply to the administration of a drug when none was indicated." And a report in the *New England Journal of Medicine* (October 17, 1974) found that "in at least 30% of hospitalized medical patients at least one adverse drug reaction develops during hospitalization. . . ."

Drugs are supposed to be prescribed only by physicians well-versed in each drug's effects, and only after an examination is performed and a thoughtful diagnosis is reached. The physician should select only the most appropriate medication available, prescribe it with clear and precise instructions that the patient understands, and follow up to be sure that the medication is being taken and is having the correct effect. When mistakes occur in the prescription of pharmaceuticals, it is usually because these basic rules were not followed.

In 1976, Dr. Harold C. Neu, then head of the division of infectious diseases at Columbia University Medical School, devised and circulated a test to determine how antibiotics were being prescribed. Of the 4,513 doctors who voluntarily took the test, only half scored better than 68 percent. Those who performed best—averaging 80 percent correct—were physicians affiliated with universities, presumably doctors with the most current information available to them. Among private family doctors, only 17 percent scored at that 80 percent level.

Antibiotics are the most misprescribed category of drug, according to statistics compiled by the National Disease and Therapeutic Index. In fact, 51 percent of the patients in this study who visited their doctors complaining of a common cold received a prescription for an antibiotic. A cold is a viral infection. Antibiotics don't work on simple cold viruses. In addition to wasting over $15 million on unnecessary medication, these patients were put at risk of possible side effects and adverse drug reactions.

Perhaps one of the reasons doctors sometimes utilize the wrong drugs is that they are no different from other consumers. Drug manufacturers spend more than $1 billion a year on advertisements in medical journals and other marketing techniques to encourage physicians to prescribe their products. Just as the general public is persuaded by advertising to buy a new car or a new laundry detergent, many doctors are enticed to try a new drug.

However, while the Federal Trade Commission, the Food and Drug Administration, and various state agencies monitor the claims in advertisements for consumer products, no one monitors the claims in drug ads marketed to doctors. There are requirements for accuracy in the advertisements that appear in medical journals, but according to a recent study written by researchers from UCLA and published in the *Annals of Internal Medicine* (June 1, 1992), the ads are not screened and most contain false information.

For instance, 92 percent of the advertisements published in medical publications failed to disclose accurately the side effects or inappropriate uses of the drugs described, which included antibiotics, hypertension drugs, antidepressants, sleeping pills, and birth control products. In the absence of this additional information, the study found, 44 percent of these ads would lead physicians to prescribe drugs incorrectly. Some ads didn't include safety information; others contained inaccurate statements about the type of patients for whom the drugs would be appropriate. And according to the study's author, in some cases, "doctors have no way to learn about many of these drugs other than the ads."

Obviously, the federal government bears some responsibility for this situation. The FDA should not allow inaccurate or misleading ads to be published. But doctors also need to be vigilant. Going back to our earlier analogy, an intelligent consumer does not buy a car based solely on its advertising. He or she does some independent research as well. Physicians need to do the same before writing a prescription for a drug that could potentially cost a patient his or her life.

As you can see, malpractice by physicians—whether in the prescription of drugs, the performance of cosmetic surgery, the diagnosis of cancer, the delivery of babies, or orthopedics—occurs under circumstances in which misconduct is plainly evident. The cases we've described are illustrative of what can be seen and heard in hospitals, doctors' offices, and courtrooms across the country. They are malpractice beyond a doubt.

In describing these "dangerous" fields of medical practice, we don't want to leave the impression that they are the only areas in which malpractice can occur. They are examples of the most prevalent forms of malpractice, but it can happen at any time, in any specialty. We also don't want to imply that every practitioner of these specialties is incompetent or prone to malpractice. In fact, the opposite is true. Despite all the negligence we have seen, the vast majority of physicians practice appropriate, excellent care.

Doctors who find themselves in the types of situations we have described, however, should think carefully about their actions and make sure they are practicing medicine in the best interests of their patients. For those patients who, for whatever reason, find themselves in such circumstances, we hope we have provided an understanding of the potential hazards and that that knowledge will help avert a catastrophe.

3

WHEN TO SUE (AND WHEN NOT TO): HOW THE LAW SEES IT

While clearly there is a great deal of malpractice in American medicine, it is also true that most doctors provide thoughtful, skillful care to their patients. We should not allow the incompetents among their ranks to make us think that all physicians are quacks. The public needs to have a better understanding of what constitutes malpractice, but part of that means understanding that doctors can't cure everything and can't make every patient happy. It is a tragic fact of medicine and life that sometimes treatments fail and sometimes patients die.

There are times when patients, out of anger or frustration or despair, blame their doctors for whatever misfortune has befallen them. Sometimes that blame is misplaced. Likewise, there are patients who bring lawsuits against their doctors unfairly. In most of those instances, the doctor and patient alike are put through an unfortunate ordeal.

Regrettably, information that would help people better assess their situations is sorely lacking, not only among the general public but among members of the medical and legal professions as well. We often receive client referrals from other doctors and lawyers—even judges—that sometimes turn out not to be true malpractice. And we reject those cases. Just as we all need to know what malpractice is, we also need to be clear about what it is not, lest we be guilty of the irresponsible actions sometimes claimed by medical and insurance industry advocates.

Every member of the legal profession should feel obligated to prevent unwarranted lawsuits. A medical malpractice suit is a serious matter. If it is unfair to the physician involved, it is also unfair to the client. If someone has been through an ordeal—been injured or suffered the loss of a loved one—it is understandable if the individual looks for someone to blame and ends up turning against the doctor. But it is terribly irresponsible for a lawyer to prey on a person in such a vulnerable position and agree to representation, knowing that there is no case. Such actions are foolish for practical as well as moral reasons: They rarely if ever prevail and they serve only to prolong the client's anguish.

One of the myths that the medical community and insurance industry perpetuate is that the malpractice crisis is nothing more than the invention of money-hungry, unscrupulous lawyers who initiate frivolous litigation against innocent doctors. With 100,000 Americans dying each year at the hands of negligent physicians, this argument is obviously false. But it's up to those of us in the legal profession to do everything possible to ensure that it remains false—that we bring to court only those cases we believe truly have merit.

Often overlooked in this debate is the biggest problem facing the American public: the vast number of patients truly victimized by doctors. Most of them never know they've been victims of malpractice, and they never sue or take other action. The Harvard study mentioned in chapter 1 estimates that in New York State as few as 3,000 lawsuits resulted from the 27,000 injuries caused by negligent medical treatment in one year. "Eight times as many patients suffer an injury from medical negligence as there are malpractice claims," according to the study. And "there are about sixteen times as many patients who suffer an injury from negligence as there are persons who receive compensation through the tort system." The report refers to other studies as well, which estimate that only one in ten instances of malpractice results in litigation. Even for those cases that result in the most severe disability or death—ones in which juries are inclined to be more sympathetic for the plaintiff—only one in seven ends in a lawsuit. And since some plaintiffs do not win their suits, only one patient receives compensation per twenty-five instances of injury from negligent care.

People who complain about frivolous suits against innocent doctors rarely discuss these statistics, and never mention the other side of the coin—the frivolous defense. Of the thousands of cases we have handled, and the thousands more with which we are familiar, we can think of very few in which the hospital or doctor involved simply came forward and admitted the mistake, apologized, and tried to accommodate the victim.

Even in the most obvious cases—where no honest person would doubt that malpractice occurred—the physicians and their insurance companies almost always deny liability, refuse responsibility, and defend against the lawsuit vigorously. No matter how many incompetent physicians are defended in court, no matter how appalling their behavior, no matter how many lives they have ruined, we have never heard a complaint from the insurance companies or professional medical associations about the time and money wasted on frivolous defenses.

Despite protestations from medical trade organizations about the "crisis" in malpractice litigation, the facts show that not only *isn't* the legal system being overwhelmed with unwarranted lawsuits, but only a small proportion of the malpractice being committed—the negligence that results in significant lawsuits—is going to court. Obviously, the public needs to be aware of what malpractice is, to recognize it when it occurs, and to understand what is required to meet the legal definition of malpractice.

Some protectors of the medical profession will surely charge that we are providing this information in an effort to spur more lawsuits. Nothing could be further from the truth. When patients are maimed or killed by an inept physician, they and their families should have legal recourse, and they should know what it is. In fact, rather than trying to drum up new business, we do exactly the opposite in our practice. We reject most prospective clients who approach us. Some of the cases we've had to decline involved clients who are physicians themselves, who simply didn't understand what malpractice is. Something has gone wrong, they are angry with their own doctor, and they want to sue. But that's not enough.

During a recent two-week period, we had an unusual experience that proves this point. Six doctors individually contacted us about filing malpractice suits against other doctors for treatment they or members of their families had received. Not one of them had a case. One was a medical school professor unhappy with his daughter's treatment by her physician. Apparently, the doctor's scheduling problems, which the patient had not anticipated, had caused the young woman to miss her college graduation ceremony, an important family dinner, and part of a vacation she had planned. However, the one thing this medical school professor failed to point out was that there had been no error in his daughter's treatment. The care she received had been fine, and she recovered perfectly. In a court of law, scheduling problems that cause inconvenience to patients—even major inconvenience—do not constitute malpractice.

Rudeness is not malpractice, either. Nor is overcharging, although that may be a crime of another kind. Nor is a nose job that doesn't come out as well as the patient expected. Neither was it malpractice, in our opinion, when a Philadelphia woman claimed that her substandard medical care had caused the loss of her psychic powers.

The law governing medical malpractice has evolved as American courts have ruled on various such issues during the past 200 years. But many of the fundamental legal guidelines date back to English common law of the eighteenth century. William Blackstone's *Commentaries*, for example, was a major source of legal insight in this area and was widely used by lawyers of the 1800s as a foundation for legal arguments that would develop into American case law on the subject. Blackstone defined malpractice as some harm to a patient's "vigor or constitution" resulting from "the neglect or unskillful management of [a] physician, surgeon or apothecary." Blackstone said that malpractice was a violation of the law because it violates the trust a patient places in his physician. The injured party could seek financial damages in court when he had shown that the accused physician, through negligence or a breach of duty, had failed to live up to his professional responsibility.

Today, lobbyists for the medical profession act as if malpractice litigation is a recent phenomenon. In fact, lawsuits against negligent physicians first became prevalent in the 1830s and 1840s. As medical and scientific advances led Americans to become less fatalistic about their health, and their lives in general, they began to place more confidence in a doctor's ability to heal injuries and cure diseases.

As American lawyers tried cases during the next century, the law became more specific. But classically, a lawsuit for medical malpractice remained nothing more than a specialized negligence action, resulting from a breach of duty by the physician. Physicians are responsible for the lives and physical well-being of their patients. Simply stated, they owe a legal duty to them, and a breach of that duty can result in civil liability.

One individual whose cases helped define the law of medical malpractice in the 1800s was an Illinois lawyer named Abraham Lincoln. In 1856, Mr. Lincoln represented two physicians who were being sued by their patient, an elderly man whom they had treated for a broken leg. The leg had shortened as it healed, leaving the man somewhat impaired. Mr. Lincoln represented his clients well, demonstrating his legendary legal prowess as he used a chicken bone to illustrate to the jury how brittle elderly bones can be. He argued that the injury might well have warranted amputation if not for the care of these doctors, whose service had indeed left the patient better off than he might otherwise have been. "The slight defect that finally resulted," he reasoned, "through Nature's methods of aiding the work of these surgeons, is nothing compared to the loss of the limb altogether." The jury ruled in favor of Mr. Lincoln's clients.

Just a few years later, though, arguing the plaintiff's side of a lawsuit, the future president won a case that would prove an important legal precedent, articulating principles that still hold true today. In this 1860 case, *Ritchey* v. *West,* in which Mr. Lincoln represented a patient who had been a victim of medical malpractice, the judge wrote in his decision:

> The principle is plain and of uniform application, that when a person assumes the profession of physician and surgeon, he must, in its exercise, be held to employ a reasonable amount of care and skill. For anything short of that degree of skill in his practice, the law will hold him responsible for any injury that may result from its absence. While he is not required to possess the highest order of qualification, to which some men may attain, still he must possess and exercise that degree of skill which is ordinarily possessed by members of the profession.

That standard—requiring physicians to possess an ordinary level of diligence, care, and skill measured against the conventions of the time and the community in which they practice—still stands today. It was further refined in an 1898 New York State case, *Pike* v. *Honsinger,* in which the court built on these previous concepts and court decisions and issued a ruling that would govern much of the law of medical malpractice into the twentieth century.

After being kicked in the knee by a horse, George Pike, a middle-aged farmer, went to the office of Dr. Willis T. Honsinger. Honsinger's son, also a physician, examined Mr. Pike and set his leg in a cast. The elder Honsinger examined Mr. Pike a week later at the patient's home and found the leg badly swollen. His diagnosis was a ruptured ligament. Although Mr. Pike continued to complain of pain and swelling over the next two months, Dr. Honsinger not only stuck to his original diagnosis but allowed the patient to resume his farm work.

Finally, Mr. Pike consulted another physician, who informed him that he had been suffering, not from a damaged ligament, but from a broken kneecap. By now, unfortunately, it was beyond repair. When Mr. Pike confronted Dr. Willis T. Honsinger and told him that he was now unable to work his farm and make a living, the doctor admitted his initial misdiagnosis and is said to have told him that "the leg was not worth a damn and he would have to go into something besides farming."

Mr. Pike sued, but despite considerable medical testimony in his favor, the trial judge refused to allow the jury to decide the case, instead directing a verdict in favor of the doctor. Mr. Pike appealed, and in its decision in his favor, the appellate court restated what it called the "well-settled" law in medical malpractice cases.

The court ruled that:

> Upon consenting to treat a patient, it becomes [the physician's] duty to use reasonable care and diligence in the exercise of his skill and the application of his learning to accomplish the purpose for which he was employed. He is under the further obligation to use his best judgment in exercising his skill and applying his knowledge. The law holds him liable for an injury to his patient resulting from want of requisite skill or knowledge or the omission to exercise reasonable care or failure to use his best judgment. The rule in relation to learning and skill does not require a surgeon to possess that extraordinary learning and skill which belong only to a few men of rare endowments, but such as is possessed by the average member of the medical profession in good standing. . . . The rule of reasonable care and diligence does not require the use of the highest possible degree of care to render a physician and surgeon liable. It is not enough that there has been a less degree of care than some other medical man might have shown or less than even he himself might have bestowed, but there must be a want of ordinary and reasonable care, leading to a bad result.

Although it broke no new legal ground, *Pike* v. *Honsinger* pulled together all the previous precedents into one clear, comprehensive decision on the responsibility of physicians to their patients and on the standards that must be met by a patient if he or she is to sue for malpractice. Most of those standards still apply today.

As a practical matter, in a modern-day lawsuit there are several areas that a patient, or plaintiff, must address in order to prove a doctor guilty of malpractice. First, as in the early malpractice suits, there must have been a departure from the normal standard of care. A case we recently declined illustrates this principle.

A sixty-one-year-old man came to us suffering from recurrent prostate cancer. His doctors had identified a cancer and had first performed surgery about two years prior to our meeting. Following the surgery, he said, there had been virtually no medical follow-up. None of the appropriate tests had been performed to determine whether the cancer had begun to recur. Eighteen months after the surgery, a CAT scan was finally performed and it showed a new lesion. The prognosis was not good.

The client retained us, we contacted the hospital, and we obtained his records. It was apparent from the records that the patient's recollection was incorrect. It is crucial for cancer patients to go through a number of regular tests, beginning immediately after surgery—in this case, blood tests for prostate-specific antigens, or PSAs. But the records showed that the PSAs had indeed been tested regularly. For most of the eighteen-month period that had passed, there had been nothing to indicate any problem. When one test showed a PSA elevation, his physician ordered a CAT scan, which found the new lesion. The patient, obviously frustrated and despondent, felt that they should have found the cancer sooner—that perhaps if they had, they would have been able to do something about it. But our cancer experts firmly believed that, while it would have been helpful to have known about the second cancer sooner, it was not reasonable to expect anyone to have located it in this case. Even if a CAT scan had been done earlier, they said, it would not have identified the lesion. There was no evidence that our client had received substandard care.

While the legal principle requiring doctors to meet a certain standard of care has been around for a long time, the term's definition has changed somewhat. In early cases, one might have argued that a physician in the Midwest could not be expected to know of scientific advances in Boston, New York, or Europe. Therefore, he was legally held to the standard that was common within a rela-

tively small, local region. Today, with improvements in communi-
cations and the broader reach of professional publications, the
standards in most communities, in most respects, should be com-
parable to those in others. Formal medical education and a physician's postgraduate study of a specialty are fairly uniform
throughout the country. A physician's basic minimum technical
skills and knowledge can be expected to meet certain standards,
regardless of where he or she is located or what facilities are at his
or her disposal. However, standards do vary in some respects, as
they should. And not all physicians in all circumstances can be
held accountable in the same way.

For example, an individual practitioner in a doctor's office in a
rural location, presented with an emergency situation, cannot be
expected to act as he would if he had immediate access to a modern medical center with the latest technology.

Usually, especially with respect to specialists—such as neurologists, orthopedic surgeons, cardiologists—courts tend to apply
national standards on the assumption that if a physician professes
to have expertise in a particular field he or she can be expected to
be up-to-date on latest treatments and technology. But there are
some exceptions. In a 1977 case, for example, a court refused to
allow the actions of an orthopedic surgeon to be measured
against the standards of the American Board of Orthopedic Surgeons because evidence had not been presented that orthopedic
surgeons in similar communities held to the same standards.

Of course, there are many times when the failure to live up to
conventional standards is obvious. For example, when an expectant mother, whether being treated in a modern medical center
or a local facility, goes into labor, her obstetrician should be there.
In some cases, however, the obstetricians lack either the time or
the interest to appear in the labor room and remain there. Then
a problem develops and the baby should be delivered as soon as
possible. Because the obstetrician isn't there, the condition is not
diagnosed promptly, action is delayed, and the baby is not delivered until after brain damage has occurred. That is a departure
from the normal standard of care.

■ ■ ■

Another requirement when a patient sues for malpractice is that he or she shows that a doctor-patient relationship existed. A patient's regular family doctor has different responsibilities from a doctor who is performing an examination for an insurance company, for instance. If a patient goes to his or her general practitioner for checkups every year and that GP fails to notice that the patient is continually coughing, or that the coughing is getting worse every year, and he fails to examine the patient for lung disease, he would probably be guilty of malpractice.

There are times when a patient is examined by a doctor with whom no such relationship exists. Someone involved in an automobile accident, for example, who suffers a broken leg and sues the other driver, may be required to have his leg examined by a physician employed by an insurance company or by the other party in the lawsuit. If the insurance company physician who examines the leg fails to detect that the patient has lung disease, that is not malpractice. The insurance company doctor has no obligation to do a thorough examination of the patient, beyond the leg injury in which his client is interested.

Legally, the physician-patient relationship is defined as a consensual relationship in which the patient knowingly seeks the assistance of the physician and the physician knowingly accepts the person as a patient. Whether or not the patient pays the doctor a fee is irrelevant. All that matters is that the patient entrusted him or herself to the care of the physician and that the physician accepted the case.

Another legal requirement for malpractice legal action is that there be some demonstrable damage caused to the patient as a result of the mistreatment. Basketball fans use the term "no harm, no foul" to describe a play in which the referee fails to call what seems to be a foul, because the foul has not prevented the player who was fouled from scoring. Fortunately in basketball "no harm, no foul" is the exception rather than the rule. In medical malpractice law, the opposite is true. If a doctor makes a mistake and is able to correct it with no lasting harm to the patient, he will generally be given the benefit of the doubt. In much the same way, someone who throws a punch but misses will never be convicted of assault. Likewise, a physician who makes a mistake but causes no serious damage will almost never be found liable for malpractice.

Finally, once it has been shown that there has been some harm done, it must also be demonstrated that the doctor's actions or inaction were a "proximate cause," or a major factor in causing that harm. The defense in medical malpractice cases often tries to show that the outcome would have been the same regardless of the treatment the patient received. The defense argues that, even if the doctor had acted differently, the patient would still have been injured or died.

For example, lung cancer takes a long time to spread—sometimes years. If a physician examines a patient, fails to detect that he has lung cancer, and the patient dies a few months later, it is difficult to prove malpractice. Given this scenario, it is likely that at the time the examination took place the cancer was already so advanced that even if he had detected it, there was probably nothing any doctor could have done to cure it.

Consider, however, the case of an internist who takes a set of chest X-rays, misreads them, and misses early signs of lung cancer in a patient. He fails to have the X-rays double-checked by a trained radiologist, either because he is lazy or because such consultations cost time and money. The patient returns a year later for another checkup, and the GP takes another chest X-ray. Again, he relies on his own ability to read X-rays, although he is not trained to do so. Again he misreads them and overlooks the cancer.

A second year passes and, during an examination by another physician, the patient discovers that he not only has lung cancer but that it is widespread and inoperable. If the first physician had caught the cancer two years earlier, either through his own examination or by consulting with a radiologist, the cancer would probably have been localized and operable. Thus, the physician's negligence was clearly a proximate cause of his patient's death. That's malpractice.

Proximate cause is an integral part of virtually every malpractice case. It is often a subject of contention and is often the most difficult element to prove to a jury. A 1974 case involving a major New York hospital illustrates how complicated it can be.

The patient, Ms. Kallenberg, was admitted to the hospital after having suffered three hemorrhages from a cerebral aneurysm, or a defect in the wall of a blood vessel in the brain. Surgery was planned. Her neurosurgeon and her general practitioner agreed that she would need to be kept on a certain medication for a period of time prior to the surgery to reduce her blood pressure and keep it relatively low. The general practitioner began to administer this medication and ordered that it be continued by the hospital staff. For some reason, these instructions were never followed. Ms. Kallenberg failed to get the medication her doctors had ordered. She died seven days after being admitted to the hospital.

The hospital's attorneys argued that the failure to administer the drugs may indeed have been an error, but they were not the cause of Ms. Kallenberg's death. There was a good chance that she would have died anyway, they said, even if she had received the prescribed medication.

The lawsuit against the hospital charged that these drugs were necessary to get Ms. Kallenberg into a condition that would allow her doctors to operate on her. Failure to provide her with her medication had caused her to deteriorate and die. Expert medical witnesses at the trial testified that this failure contributed to her death. Had she received the medication, and had she successfully undergone surgery, she would have had up to a 40 percent chance of survival. Even without the surgery, had she received this medication, she would have had some—albeit slight—chance of recovery.

The judge ruled that this was a question for the jury to decide, and it did, in favor of Ms. Kallenberg's family. The court said that what had to be shown to prove proximate cause was that the patient "might" have improved sufficiently to undergo surgery and make a recovery. A later court ruling clarified this principle further in stating that the doctor or hospital's action or inaction could be seen as a proximate cause of the death or injury if "there was a substantial possibility the decedent would have recovered but for the malpractice."

Another case that presents some similar legal issues involved Julia Rudolfsky, a single mother pregnant with her second child, expecting to deliver at a major metropolitan medical center with an excellent reputation.

Ms. Rudolfsky's first child was delivered by cesarean section, necessitated by a condition known as placenta previa. This condition, in which the placenta is located over the cervix, always causes hemorrhaging and makes a natural delivery impossible. She had informed her obstetrician about her earlier cesarean from the start, although she was fuzzy about the medical reasons for its having been needed. Her doctor, Allen Ruben, examined her carefully, though, and told her not to worry. In fact, he said, there was a chance that no C-section would be needed this time—a natural delivery might be possible. Dr. Ruben had been recommended to her by friends. He was associated with an excellent hospital, and Ms. Rudolfsky went through her pregnancy feeling very confident.

When she reached term—on her exact due date, in fact—she visited Dr. Ruben in his office. He performed a sonogram, told her everything was fine, and sent her home. She was not ready yet, he said; she would have to wait a bit longer.

Two weeks later, she returned. He examined her again and this time found evidence of some bleeding. "Don't worry," he said. "Go home and rest. You're not ready yet."

Two weeks later, Ms. Rudolfsky placed an urgent call to her doctor. She was hemorrhaging. At this point, he finally advised her to go to the hospital. She arrived at the emergency room bleeding severely. A resident examined her and treated her no differently from any routine admission. It took about twenty minutes for the hospital to make up her room, after which she was left to wait for Dr. Ruben. And wait. And wait.

Two hours later, Dr. Ruben, who lived only a short distance from the hospital, arrived. He found his patient still hemorrhaging and now in shock from the drastic loss of blood. He finally performed the cesarean section, but the damage was done. By the time he got around to delivering this baby, the mother had been bleeding for weeks and had gone into shock. Her child was delivered to her severely and permanently brain-damaged.

Dr. Ruben had known of her previous cesarean. He had known that she had previously had a placenta previa. Any competent physician would have treated this as a high-risk case, expecting a recurrence of the condition. Any competent physician would have seen from the sonogram that the condition had indeed recurred. Any competent physician would have planned to perform a C-section at some point close to term, before the mother went into labor, thus avoiding the inevitable complications.

What legal question could there possibly be in such an obvious case of negligence? Clearly, a doctor-patient relationship existed. Ms. Rudolfsky had been seeing Dr. Ruben regularly for six months and he had agreed to deliver her baby. Clearly, there was serious harm to the patient and her child. The baby is severely mentally retarded and will never be able to live a normal life. The mother will now have to spend the rest of her life taking care of him, and worrying about how he'll be taken care of after she's gone.

There is no doubt that Dr. Ruben failed to treat Ms. Rudolfsky with anything approaching the normal standard of care. And it is obvious that this substandard treatment was a proximate cause of the tragic injury to the fetus. However, in our lawsuit, we charged not only Dr. Ruben with malpractice but the hospital as well. When a woman who is almost ten months pregnant arrives at a hospital hemorrhaging, she should not simply be admitted and left bleeding in a bed for two and a half hours until her doctor arrives.

The hospital argued that its actions were not a proximate cause of the injury. It said that its treatment of the patient was not an issue, that regardless of what it had done, the result would have been the same. The mistakes had been made, the damage had been done, prior to her arrival at their emergency room.

We disagreed. The hospital should not have taken almost half an hour to admit her, and it should not have left her waiting for her incompetent doctor to arrive. If necessary, a senior resident in obstetrics in the hospital should have been called upon to perform the cesarean—immediately. The two and a half hours that Ms. Rudolfsky lay bleeding might have made a big difference in the future of her child.

We were successful in making our point. The lawsuit was settled for more than a $1.3 million.

As you can see, screening and selection of clients in malpractice cases requires great care. When this screening is done properly, it can effectively avoid unnecessary lawsuits. Physicians and medical associations scream about frivolous lawsuits in cases where the physicians and hospitals involved have done nothing but exert their best efforts on behalf of an unfortunate patient. They argue that lawyers work on contingency fees—that clients don't have to pay any legal fees unless they win the case, so they have a great incentive to sue regardless of the merits of the case.

Well, those are the uninformed arguments of people who have never practiced law. We discuss this subject at length in chapter 7, but the contingency fees provide access to the courts for people who otherwise would be unable to afford it. Ms. Rudolfsky didn't have a lot of money. She was faced with a lifetime of bills to pay for her son's care. Had she had to pay a lawyer an hourly retainer whether she won or lost her case, she might never have sued. And she would have been left with nothing.

Second, contingency fees actually are protection against frivolous lawsuits. Malpractice cases are complex and almost always contentious. They take hundreds of hours of work and sometimes are not resolved for years. Under those circumstances, no reputable attorney is going to take a case and exert that kind of effort if he doesn't truly believe the case has merit.

Our firm has a rigorous screening process for prospective cases and prospective clients. We believe our methods are unusual and hope that they may prove enlightening to physicians and lawyers who have been involved in malpractice cases, as well as to ordinary people.

We are presented with more than 100 potential cases each week; of those, we accept an average of three. The other ninety-seven for the most part are troubling. Often these people have been through tremendous suffering, and it is hard to turn them away. But if we don't believe they have been victims of actual malpractice, there's not much we can do.

Most often, the first step in the process is a phone interview. We are contacted by between twenty and thirty prospective clients per day, all of whom are screened initially, either by phone or in person, by a highly trained individual with a Ph.D. in nursing, who compiles a history including all the details of the treatment and the condition.

Many callers are vague or simply don't remember important dates and details at first, making it difficult to form an initial judgment about the case, but at this stage we rely on our experience and instinct. Sometimes it's clear from the outset that no real problem exists. Some people have not suffered any injury at all; they simply are angry with their physician about his bill or attitude or personality. Some callers aren't sure themselves whether they want to sue and are really looking for information and guidance.

Each week, we review the cases of those who seem to have legitimate grievances. After careful consideration, we usually discover that about 10 to 15 percent merit proceding further. We then meet with these potential clients in person and interview them carefully in an effort to learn all we can about their cases. After these interviews, we usually find that we are left about 5 or 6 percent of those we started with.

We view the screening process as one of the most important parts of our practice. It's more complex than most people would assume, and it is often quite time-consuming. The interviewing of clients and the investigation of their claims are a science that requires both patience and experience. Possibly because of our personal medical backgrounds, we conduct this process in a way not dissimilar from how a physician examines and diagnoses patients.

Our personal interviews are usually extremely thorough, as we probe deeply into the relevant details of the client's case. Often, as in medical diagnosis, the client is not the best judge of what is important. When a good doctor takes a medical history, he or she spends a long time listening to the patient's story, asking careful, probing questions. Sometimes a patient will describe at length what he believes to be his health problem, going on about incidents and symptoms that later prove to be irrelevant. Then, at the end, he will mention something in passing that seems trivial, and it proves to be the key to the illness.

Also, the clients who come to us, whether they themselves or members of their family have been victimized, often don't know exactly what happened to them. When you go to the doctor, you don't plan on anything going wrong and you don't plan on having to sue some day. So most people don't keep track of details. Sometimes they think something happened that didn't. Sometimes their recollection is faulty. They've been told certain things by their doctors, or by the staff at the hospital. Maybe it's true, maybe it isn't. Usually, they have not seen their medical records. Even if they have, it might not have meant much to them. Good doctors need to be good detectives, and so do good lawyers.

Cancer patients often complain about the effects of their chemotherapy, when what's important are the precise date they first noticed symptoms, when they informed their doctor, what tests the doctor performed at what point. Parents may think that their brain-damaged child was injured during labor, when in fact it was after he was born. It's still a problem, it may still be malpractice, but for different reasons than the parent originally thought.

The reasons for deciding not to take a case are almost as varied as the cases themselves, but they tend to fall into several categories. Treatment dates are among the first things we look at. Often patients do not realize that they've been victims of malpractice until years after the incident has occurred. Sometimes, the statute of limitations, which says that after a certain period of time has passed you can no longer sue, has expired. In New York State, for example, while there are certain exceptions, the statute of limitations is two and a half years from the time the malpractice occurred, and ten years if the victim was a minor. In Ohio, it is one year from the cognizable event—the point at which the victim had first had the ability to know that malpractice took place. The statute of limitations varies from state to state and from case to case, and can depend upon such factors as (1) whether the hospital is operated privately or by a city, state, or the federal government; (2) in which municipality the malpractice occurs; and (3) whether the suit involves a wrongful death action. These statutes of limitations, which are sometimes as short as ninety days, often prevent true malpractice victims from bringing lawsuits.

There are other cases, as well, in which the treatment dates prove to be keys to the viability of the case. A fifty-three-year-old woman retained us while in the midst of a terrible situation. She said that she had been going to the same doctor for twenty years and that she had been examined regularly. She said that years earlier, the doctor had found a lump on her breast, diagnosed it as benign, aspirated it (took a sample of fluid or tissue for analysis) as he should have, and told her not to worry. He never recommended that the patient have a mammogram. One day during a self-examination, she found on her breast a lump that was quite large. She returned to her physician who, this time, did order a mammogram. The mammogram confirmed the presence of a tumor. The diagnosis after further tests was stage three breast cancer. The prognosis was bleak—the patient would probably die.

A very sad story and, on its face, a case of unbelievable medical negligence. When we obtained her medical records, however, we found that, in recounting her story to us, she had overlooked a crucial detail. It was true that she had begun seeing this doctor twenty years ago. It was true that he had found a lump and diagnosed it as benign without sending his patient for a mammogram. That, in and of itself, is substandard care: She should have had a mammogram. But in examining the treatment dates in the patient's medical files, we realized that for two years prior to discovery of the cancer, she had not been to see the doctor at all. Two years is a long time. It's enough time to develop stage three breast cancer.

It's possible that the version of events as this client presented them were correct. It's possible that her physician misdiagnosed her as a result of his failure to have a mammogram done. It's possible that she developed a fatal case of cancer as a result. But there is no way of proving it in a court of law.

The doctor would argue that, while perhaps a mammogram should have been done, his initial diagnosis was correct. The lump he examined was benign. This cancer, he would argue, only began to develop during the two years in which he had not seen the patient. While we could claim that she had received substandard care, there would have been no way of demonstrating that that care—rather than the patient's own negligence in putting off an examination—had been the cause of this woman's condition.

Delays in the diagnosis and treatment of cancer are part of many cases we see and, unfortunately, many of the cases we reject. As we've said, even though the medical treatment may have been negligent, it may not have altered the ultimate outcome. It may not have been a proximate cause of the patient's illness or death.

We need to be able to prove that the doctor knew about the cancer—or should have known—early enough to have prevented it from taking its toll. A fifty-one-year-old woman and her husband consulted us several years ago in such a case. In August 1987 she detected a lump on her breast during a self-examination. She did nothing about it, though, until it caused painful swelling two months later. Her physician aspirated the lump, ordered a sonogram, diagnosed it as benign, and prescribed penicillin. They scheduled another appointment for three weeks later, at which time another sonogram was taken. The doctor said he had no reason to change his diagnosis and told the patient to return in six months.

The following January, five months after initially finding the lump on her breast, the patient's husband changed his health insurance coverage. She decided to make an appointment with a different physician, one who participated in the new insurance plan. This doctor not only ordered a sonogram but a mammogram as well. His diagnosis, confirmed by a biopsy, was malignant breast cancer. A week later, a mastectomy was performed.

The first doctor had obviously misread the sonogram. He also probably erred in not sending his patient for a mammogram. But the time that had passed was not really significant. For the cancer to have been as advanced in January as it turned out to be, it must almost certainly have also been at a stage in October that would have required a mastectomy to be performed anyway. This woman was outraged with that first doctor, and rightly so. It was grossly incompetent for him to prescribe penicillin and send her home for six months in her condition. But we had to let her know, as difficult as it was, that under the law we would not be able to prove malpractice. Even if the doctor had diagnosed the cancer competently and correctly from the outset, the result would probably have been the same.

Sometimes, after investigating a case thoroughly and interviewing the client at length, we find evidence that the patient may have contributed to his or her own condition. Perhaps he or she ignored a doctor's advice, failed to take prescribed medication, refused to be hospitalized when it was required, or would not submit to a necessary diagnostic test. Patients cannot sue when their doctors give them good advice and they don't follow it.

Our in-person interviews often turn up points that we'd be unable to determine over the phone and that lead to rejection of certain clients. One man told us on the phone that he was unable to move his right arm. When he came to our office, he introduced himself with a firm handshake. That was the end of that case.

One of the areas we tend to avoid in general is cosmetic surgery, and that is for practical reasons more than legal ones. The only clients we accept whose complaint involves plastic surgery—and there have been a number of them—are those who have sustained injuries that are obviously serious. Juries are unsympathetic toward plaintiffs whose only complaint is that they don't like the way their nose looks or thought a face lift would make them look younger. There are some cases we've seen, though, where incompetent plastic surgeons caused permanent scarring and injury. In one case, a patient died undergoing surgery on her nose. We've already discussed the culpability of plastic surgeons who used silicon breast implants for cosmetic reasons. Of course, plastic surgeons who have done serious harm to their patients deserve to have the book thrown at them, and we have no reservation about doing just that.

Among the types of cases we are particularly concerned about are ones involving patients at either end of the age spectrum—children and the elderly. Not all attorneys share this view because, callous as it may seem, elderly clients do not receive large awards. Insurance companies will claim, and juries will often agree, that because they have fewer years of life ahead of them, elderly people are entitled to lesser amounts of money, regardless of the severity of the malpractice against them. But we take these cases as a matter of conscience and we litigate them vigorously.

After our personal interviews we are left with only those few cases—about 5 percent of what we started with—that we feel are just. But we recognize that, even at this point, further examination may prove us wrong.

When we sign a retainer agreement with a client, we let the individual know that this is only the beginning of our investigative process. This agreement enables us to obtain medical records from the client's physicians and hospital. We research these records; even with our own medical expertise, we often send them to outside medical experts for further evaluation. Sometimes the records show that, despite the client's recollection, there was no malpractice. At other times—just as it takes doctors to commit malpractice—it takes medical experts to determine whether or not it has actually occurred.

James Goldfield is a rather elderly man who has been plagued for over forty years with a condition called osteomyelitis, a chronic bone infection. In January 1990, Mr. Goldfield began complaining of some pain and his physician, a vascular surgeon, recommended débridement of the area, a fairly common procedure in such cases. Débridement is usually performed in an operating room because sterile surroundings are required, but the surgery is simple, involving merely cleaning out the infected tissue in the area along with any dead skin and bone. Mr. Goldfield was monitored regularly after this procedure as an outpatient in his doctor's office.

The area seemed to be healing for a while, but in June it once again became infected. Another débridement was performed. This time, however, the doctor found more than infected tissue—he found a tumor, which a biopsy determined was malignant. Further tests found it to be spreading. In July, the leg was amputated.

Some time later, Mr. Goldfield discovered a lab report, based on the first débridement procedure performed six months earlier, that showed the presence of cancerous cells. Apparently there had been some delay by the hospital in producing this report and making it available to either Mr. Goldfield or his doctor. The lab analysis had been done in a timely fashion, but apparently no one in this busy hospital had time to type it up and distribute it. If the doctor had had this vital information five months earlier, Mr. Goldfield thought, they might have been able to save his leg.

A clear-cut case where avoidable delay in diagnosis resulted in serious harm to the patient? As it turned out, no. This case was extremely difficult to unravel and required even more investigation and medical evaluation than usual.

Mr. Goldfield had severe vascular problems, with very poor circulation in his leg. Surgery is a risky undertaking for such patients because they don't have enough blood circulating to heal the wound that surgery causes. When we went beyond the facts and looked into Mr. Goldfield's history, we realized that he would not have been a candidate for the type of limited cancer surgery he had envisioned. Even if his surgeon had had those early tests results in a timely fashion, he could not have performed surgery on Mr. Goldfield as he would have on the average patient. Even if he had known about the cancer five months earlier, before it had begun to spread, the leg would still have had to be removed.

In this case, we would have been able to show easily that the hospital had not lived up to the normal standard of care. Hospitals should be expected to provide their doctors with the results of tests they order without undue delay. But we could not show that the substandard care—the delay in diagnosis—was a proximate cause of the loss of Mr. Goldfield's leg. Inexcusable as this delay was, the patient was no worse for it than he would otherwise have been.

We have tried to provide some perspective on how the law sees medical malpractice—when to sue and when not to sue. However, just because someone does not have a good legal case—one that will prevail in a court of law—does not mean he or she received good medical care. That is an important distinction, and one that everyone from medical providers to medical consumers should focus on. According to the American legal system, in a court of law the burden is on the plaintiff to prove that malpractice occurred. That is as it should be, but sometimes it's a difficult task.

Whether or not a physician is legally liable for malpractice is a complicated question, but it's usually clear whether he or she has practiced good medicine or bad medicine. Doctors who have delayed, misdiagnosed, or otherwise mistreated their patients should not feel satisfaction knowing that they are not legally liable. The best physicians do not examine, diagnose, or treat patients with an eye toward what is required to avoid being sued. The best physicians direct efforts toward providing the best treatment possible for their patients. Doctors and patients alike should insist on nothing less.

4

THERE OUGHT TO BE A LAW

Although she was born in the United States in 1917, shortly after her parents arrived in this country from Poland, Rena Menska could easily have passed for an immigrant herself. She was a simple woman with simple tastes, and she seemed always to carry a bit of the old country with her, perhaps as a tribute to the memory of her parents.

Family was important to Ms. Menska, and the fact that she'd never married, never had any children of her own, made her cling all the more tightly to her older brother William and his family, particularly his two sons. She had lived all her life in Brooklyn as had they, but when William decided that the old neighborhood wasn't safe anymore, she reluctantly packed her things and moved with him to a big house in Connecticut. She didn't like feeling dependent on her brother, but she knew that she needed to be close to him and his family and that this was the only way. She would insist on helping to take care of the children and the house, though, as a way of pitching in.

Ms. Menska had seen many changes during her long lifetime—many scientific advances, from the invention of television to the advent of space travel. She marveled at the America we know today, but in some ways she was wary of it. She never used the

76

microwave and she didn't like to fly. Sometimes the old ways were better, she thought.

She had been generally quite healthy her entire life. She was never one to complain about the minor aches and ailments of old age. When she began to feel some pain and discomfort in her rectum, she ignored it for a while, certain that it was nothing to worry about. When she noticed some blood in her stool, however, she decided to see her doctor, Steven Berg.

Dr. Berg reassured her that, indeed, it was probably nothing. He examined her, found two sizable hemorrhoids, which, he said, were common in women her age. As a precaution, he recommended that she undergo a sigmoidoscopy to examine the inside of the rectal cavity more carefully, and a barium enema. These tests are used to uncover cancers that are not always visible during an examination. Both tests were performed over the next two months and both were negative. Dr. Berg prescribed suppositories for the hemorrhoids, and asked Ms. Menska to return in four months for another examination. At that time, Ms. Menska reported that she was feeling fine. An examination showed that the hemorrhoids were no longer present.

About a year later the pain and bleeding returned, but she didn't worry about it. She scheduled another appointment with Dr. Berg, assuming that her hemorrhoids had returned and that the doctor would prescribe some more suppositories to clear up the problem. The examination did not go as she had planned.

Dr. Berg did indeed feel the presence of a lump, but this time it was the size of a walnut and he didn't think it was a hemorrhoid. He referred her to a surgeon to have the mass biopsied. The biopsy results were positive. The unthinkable had happened. She was diagnosed with the disease that she previously had spoken about only in whispers. Rena Menska had colon cancer.

When Dr. Berg told her the bad news, he could see how hard it had hit her. Obviously, she had seen a lot of people die of cancer over the years. She now thought that this disease was about to claim her life as well. But the doctor stressed that the cancer had been caught fairly early, that she had a number of options, that patients in her position usually had an excellent chance of survival. In fact, surgery and follow-up treatment almost always provided a cure. She should not assume the worst, he told her. She should check into the hospital for further tests to determine exactly what course of treatment would be best. For the most part, he talked and she listened. She didn't ask many questions. He wasn't sure he was getting through to her, so he called the hospital while she was still there to make arrangements for her admission two days later. He handed her a note with the date and the name of the hospital.

Ms. Menska went home that afternoon feeling depressed. She would have to tell her brother and his wife the news when they got home. But what would she tell them? That she was going to the hospital? That she had cancer? That she was going to die? She turned on the radio, but only half-listened as she sat in the kitchen, immersed in thought. She was startled back into focus as she realized that they were talking on the radio about cancer. Someone was on, a doctor they said—Emanuel Revici—talking about a different type of treatment he had developed for cancer. He was speaking about how the conventional treatments that most doctors and hospitals use don't really work—in fact, they often make things worse. His treatment didn't require surgery. He used medications with which he had got excellent results in reducing the size of tumors and curing cancer completely. When Revici gave his phone number, Ms. Menska wrote it down eagerly.

That evening after dinner, she told William everything that had happened. He was of the same generation, and he reacted with the same shock and despair she had felt earlier. She told him that she had an appointment at the hospital, but that she had heard on the radio about another doctor who had a different type of treatment. She was thinking of making an appointment with him instead. William thought it made sense. Why not at least get a second opinion?

The next day, she called Dr. Berg to cancel her appointment to be admitted to the hospital. He was very concerned and advised her not to cancel. It was likely that surgery was necessary, he told her, and the sooner the better. At the moment, her prognosis was excellent, but a delay could have terrible consequences. He hoped she would not wait too long. That was the last conversation Dr. Berg had with her. That same day, she took the train to Manhattan to see Mr. Revici.

Emanuel Revici, a native of Romania, claimed to have received his medical degree at the Institute de Pharmacia y Medicine in Bucharest in 1920. He continued to study, do research, and write in Romania for the next decade, at which time he emigrated to France, where he says he obtained a position at a well-known research institute. Cancer research was his passion, and he claims to have devoted much of his time in France to experimentation and study in this area.

In 1941, he moved to Mexico, where he founded the Institute of Applied Biology, and continued to experiment and study the causes and treatments of cancer. His Mexican research marks a significant point in his life, since it was then that he sought to make a breakthrough in cancer therapy through the use of human and animal placentas in the treatment of tumors. Unfortunately, he now says, he was unable to obtain a sufficient supply of placentas to complete this research. During Revici's stay in Mexico, he began to attract attention in the United States, and began seeing American patients who were lured south of the border by the hope of a miracle. In 1945, nine American doctors went to Mexico to investigate the Revici methods firsthand, and when they returned to this country they reported on their impressions in a letter to the *Journal of the American Medical Association* (August 18, 1945):

> Personal investigations reveal a modernistic building for hospitalization with inadequate laboratory or other scientific facilities. The physician in charge has a courteous and considerate bedside manner. We think that he makes his patients feel better by virtue of his personality. There is no positive evidence that he or his associates are successful by their peculiar methods in interrupting the usual course of a malignant process.

The theoretical bases for the method of treatment are extraordinary. While they make use of current scientific concepts, they are not in accord in any way with established biochemical or pathological considerations. . . .

A characteristic but unfortunate aspect of this matter is that no satisfactory clinical records are kept. Various statements are made from time to time in notebooks, but no attempt has been made, as far as we know, to provide clinical records that would be at all acceptable for clinical appraisal according to modern standards.

It is concluded that little benefit may result from cancer patients going to Mexico City for this new "treatment."

Put simply, this American medical team's conclusion was a total indictment of Revici. His techniques, they said, represented an "extraordinary" deviation from the normal standards of medical care, he kept no records to verify his claims, and he could produce no evidence that any of his treatments worked.

With those inauspicious notices, in 1947, Revici emigrated to the United States, obtained a license to practice medicine, and opened the New York office of the Institute of Applied Biology. In 1961, he wrote a book which detailed his views on cancer therapy. Published by a vanity press, paid for by Revici's institute, the theories advanced in this book amounted to nothing more than chemical gibberish.

In essence, Revici apparently believed that cancer—and virtually every other disease—is the result of energy imbalances and its evolution can be altered by bringing the body into balance chemically. Once the presence of cancer had been determined, he would take blood and urine specimens from his patients on three successive days, and through these specimens, he believed he could determine the nature of their imbalance. In addition to testing the pH of his patients' urine, he also studied its surface tension, measuring the rate at which it evaporated, apparently believing that these tests were in some way related to the presence of cancer. It is an understatement to say that the theories are baseless.

Revici used a number of drugs in his cancer treatment, including selenium, most of which were combinations he had invented. Sometimes patients brought their urine samples to his office, so that he could determine the proper dosage of these medications. Other times, he would give them paper strips to bring home, with which they could test their own urine and regulate their own medication. None of the medications he used were ever tested or approved by the Food and Drug Administration.

When patients went to receive the Revici miracle cure, they did so through the not-for-profit Institute of Applied Biology. Rather than pay Revici a fee for his services or for the medication he provided, they made a donation to the institute. The institute, in turn, paid Revici. No money ever went to him directly from patients, thus he was able to claim the mantle of humanitarianism, telling patients and the public that he took no fee from patients for his work. Of course, he also used this guise to skirt the law, claiming that, since he was not selling his unapproved drugs—not marketing them commercially, but giving them to patients for free—he was not required to obtain FDA approval.

Three times over the years, the *Journal of the American Medical Association* warned of the risks of the Revici method of cancer treatment. In 1949, the *Journal* said that a "vague form of alleged cancer therapy . . . is that attributed to Emanuel Revici, said to be a refugee physician from Romania. The history of the 'treatment' promoted by this person begins in Mexico City, where patients from the United States were attracted by claims of a new method. . . . Subsequently, Revici spent a few months at the University of Chicago, where he was given an opportunity to demonstrate his method, with the result that in 52 patients with cancer no favorable effects could be attributed to this form of therapy."

In 1965, after he'd been practicing in New York for eighteen years, a comprehensive study followed thirty-three of his patients from the time their treatment began. With the exception of two patients whom the researchers eventually lost track of, all either died or were near death as the study concluded. The *Journal of the American Medical Association* (October 18, 1965) concluded:

> No instance of objective tumor regression was observed in any of the 33 patients studied; necropsies [autopsies] in 15 cases likewise failed to demonstrate gross or microscopic evidence of tumor alteration as a consequence of therapy.

> Based on the above-mentioned cases, the Clinical Appraisal
> Group is forced to conclude that [this] method of treatment
> of cancer is without value.

Despite these terrible reviews by the medical community, this individual continued to offer his treatment to the public—indeed, he actively promoted himself and his cure in the media. In addition, while he was seeing cancer patients through the institute, he began treating heroin addicts at a small hospital he founded—Trafalgar Hospital—where he used many of the same methods as for his cancer patients, plus another unusual treatment he called bionaire. The linguistic derivation of *bionaire* is "living air," but no one was ever able to determine the medical derivation, probably because it is a total fraud. The hospital ran into some problems in the 1970s, however. The care of virtually all the heroin-addicted patients was being paid by Medicaid, and after paying fees for more than 2,000 patients to receive worthless selenium and bionaire treatments, New York State decided it was not going to continue. It cut off payments to Revici and the hospital soon closed. He sold the building to developers, who converted it into a luxury condominium. But nothing ever happened to Revici. Even though the state had determined that his treatments were not viable and that it was no longer going to pay for them, it did nothing to stop him from seeing patients privately.

Rena Menska didn't read medical publications. She didn't know about heroin patients. She listened to the radio, though, and they wouldn't put a doctor on the radio if he wasn't good, would they?

Revici saw Ms. Menska, although what constituted his examination is questionable. He reviewed the copies she had brought with her of her biopsy results and other medical records, and he made a note of the findings in his own records. He never contacted any of those doctors. He never checked her pulse or her heart rate, or performed the other procedures that are part of a normal examination.

But doctor and patient hit it off from the start. Not cold like many younger doctors she had seen, Revici had a warm manner that reassured the nervous patient. He told her about his research in Europe, Mexico, and America and his demeanor appealed to Ms. Menska's Old World sensibilities. It was a good thing she had come to him, he said. Surgery would have been a terrible mistake. He described his theories about imbalances of energy in the body and explained that, by making incisions in the body, surgery often causes these imbalances to spread. He warned her against proceeding with that sort of treatment and convinced her to place herself in his care.

He gave her a supply of T-Sel, a selenium mixture he had concocted, and other so-called medications along with a kit to use at home to test her urine. From time to time she was to telephone him to tell him the results of the urine test, and he would determine how she was doing and what dosage of medication to take. She continued her regular contact with Revici over the course of the next year and a half, seeing him or speaking with him by phone almost weekly. She continued taking her medication as ordered.

After approximately four months, this "doctor" told Ms. Menska and noted in his records that she was "well, better." He continued telling her of significant progress and improvement over the months that followed, with notes in his files of "better," and "much better." During this time he made copious notes reflecting on the color of the patient's urine and repeatedly told her that the tumor was shrinking. After about nine months, he told her that the tumor had almost completely disappeared.

Later that month, at a Christmas gathering of relatives, several members of the family noticed that Rena Menska didn't seem well. They noticed a strong body odor emanating from this woman who had always been so fastidious. At one point during the evening, her nephew Arthur followed her upstairs and found her in the bedroom, trembling and feverish. As the trembling soon turned to convulsions, he picked her up, carried her downstairs, and brought her to the hospital.

At the hospital, they found a massive tumor of the colon, located at its lower end only one and a half inches from the anal verge. Further examination showed it to have spread to the vaginal wall. The physicians at the hospital recommended immediate surgery, but the patient insisted on speaking with Revici before consenting. After reaching him by phone, she discharged herself from the hospital, against the strong protestations of the hospital's physicians.

The doctor who treated her made this notation in her chart:

> [The patient] is a sixty-three year old white female with a rectal mass first documented in March of 1982 who has been treated in New York City by a physician named Revici. He has been treating her with an unproven method of cancer treatment called H530 which is a liquid which she drinks. A phone call to this physician elicited the information that this was selenium. The American Cancer Society was contacted who furnished us with a long sheet about Revici. He has been using this unproven method of cancer treatment for approximately 20 years. He has been investigated several times and there has been no documented response in any patient from his method of cancer treatment. He has claimed that he has cured her of cancer. . . .
>
> Despite many conversations, the patient signed herself out against medical advice because he urged her not to cooperate with any of the tests. Since her discharge, I have filed charges against Revici with the New York County and New York State Medical Society.

Revici apparently persuaded Rena Menska that hospitals are no good for her, that the surgery these physicians were recommending would do her more harm than good, that she was much better off getting out of the hospital and putting herself back into his hands. She believed in him and she followed his instructions to the letter.

Three months later, she reported to Revici that feces were coming through her vagina uncontrollably. Obviously, the cancer had torn through the wall between the rectum and the vagina. At this point, even Revici recognized that the patient needed surgery and he referred her to a surgeon with whom he was familiar at another hospital. The purpose of the surgery, he said, was simply to repair the tear, or fistula, that had developed. And while a portion of the tumor was removed during this operation, the surgeon found that it had already affected several organs and would be impossible to remove completely.

Once again, the patient was discharged into the care of her trusted Revici. The first time seeing the patient after her hospitalization, he told her that she was doing better. In May, fourteen months after first meeting Ms. Menska, he told her that the lesion was smaller.

In August, she was admitted again on an emergency basis to the first hospital. Cancer was determined to be present in her colon, rectum, and vagina. There were multiple masses in her liver. There was nothing that could be done. Her family was told that she had approximately six months to live. Against their advice, she left the hospital, returned to Revici, and continued seeing him regularly. He prescribed antibiotics for what he said was an infection.

Rena Menska died in November. The autopsy revealed cancer of her skin, bone, liver, and lung. She had died in severe pain, after many months of suffering, as the cancer literally ripped through parts of her body and her bowel movements became uncontrollable. The final notations in Revici's files on this patient stated "The patient has had radiation treatment in the back. . . . She had consequently radiation burns . . . heavily infected . . . also with an abscess to be opened. . . . Apparently she made a septicemia of which she died." In other words, he concluded that this patient, whose body was found riddled with cancer, who might well have been cured had she had surgery a year earlier, died as a result of an infection caused by radiation treatment she received at the hospital. This notation, however, was dated October 17, a full month before the patient died.

We knew Revici very well. Two years earlier, another of his former patients—this one fortunate enough to still be alive—approached us. Dorothy Samuels had a lump on her breast that had been diagnosed as malignant. Her physician strongly recommended immediate surgery. But she heard a "doctor" on the radio and agreed with his philosophy about a more holistic approach to medicine. She wanted to avoid surgery and thought that his unconventional approach was a better way to go.

Revici treated Ms. Samuels with his selenium concoction for about ten months, from February through the end of the year. Then, by coincidence, at a New Year's party, Ms. Samuels mentioned to a family member who happened to be a physician that she was seeing Revici. She told him how this great doctor was curing her. She described how he had told her the lump in her breast was becoming softer.

The physician immediately became concerned and insisted on examining her on the spot. They went upstairs to her bedroom, and his cursory examination revealed that the tumor in her breast had grown so large that it was actually beginning to break through the skin. If indeed it had become softer, it was only because the tumor had overgrown the blood supply in the breast and cells had begun to die. But rather than being cured, as Revici had claimed, it had grown and was continuing to grow.

At this point Ms. Samuels at last lost faith, accepted her relative's advice, and checked into the hospital. Once she did, more extensive testing revealed that the cancer had not only virtually filled up one breast but had crossed the midline and spread to the other as well. A double mastectomy was required, followed by months of chemotherapy and radiation therapy. Dorothy Samuels's life was saved, thanks to the chance intervention of a family member who happened to be at her New Year's Eve party.

Further, Ms. Samuels would have had a good chance of avoiding the mastectomy completely had she undergone more limited surgery when it was originally recommended. Certainly she would not have lost both breasts. The "care" this patient received had nearly cost her her life.

Here was a doctor who had been denounced by the medical community, whose treatments had been disparaged in the medical journals, against whom complaints had been filed with the state. Yet he continued to practice medicine, continued to appear on radio and television talk shows promoting his cure, and continued to prey on desperate patients.

When the Menska family came to us, we prepared another lawsuit against him, and filed it this time in Federal District Court. Since Ms. Menska had been a resident of Connecticut and Revici's practice was in New York, he was engaging in interstate commerce. This gave us the ability to try the case in Federal Court, where the calendar is less crowded and trials proceed more swiftly than in state courts.

As we investigated this case, we found a number of bizarre occurrences, some of which involved Revici's record-keeping practices, which we will discuss later. Most interesting, however, was what happened when, at our suggestion, the State Health Department searched its files in an attempt to locate a medical degree for this individual. What they found was a fuzzy photocopy of what was purported to be a diploma from the Institute de Pharmacia y Medicine in Bucharest. This document seemed questionable to the state officials, but when they asked Revici to produce the original, they were told that he didn't have it, that he'd given it to the state earlier, at its request, a statement which the state denied. We attempted to contact the institute in Bucharest, but were told that records going back to the 1920s had been destroyed during World War II. We questioned him about his background during the trial—his training, his alleged research here and abroad—and his answers were hardly satisfactory. The article in the *Journal of the American Medical Association* (January 8, 1949) referred to his work at the University of Chicago, but when we asked him under oath, he admitted to spending about one day at the university. When we asked him about his research in France, it became clear that he had fabricated that as well.

Since that time, we have suspected that Revici is not a doctor of medicine at all. His unbelievable lack of knowledge about medical matters, which we also pressed him on at the trial, certainly supports this theory. The institute he says he graduated from granted degrees in both medicine and pharmacology. And while we have no proof, judging by his obsession with developing new drug concoctions he may well have graduated as a pharmacist. If that is the case, "Dr." Revici is one of the greatest con men in history.

In any event, Revici fought the lawsuit, and while admitting that his treatment deviated from the normal standard of care for a cancer patient, contended unflinchingly that his treatment was *superior* to the standard. Needless to say, the court did not agree with his assessment and found him to be liable for the wrongful death of his patient. The jury awarded a verdict of $1.3 million to the Menska family.

Shortly after that verdict, and largely as a result of the publicity that attended the trial, the New York State Health Department—which is responsible for physician discipline in the state—responded to the complaint filed by Ms. Menska's nephew and charged Revici with fraudulent practice, gross incompetence, and gross negligence. End of story? An incompetent physician uncovered and drummed out of the medical profession in shame? Hardly.

The State Board of Regents—the state body that licenses and revokes the licenses of physicians—overruled the Health Department's recommendation and allowed this individual who could not even produce a medical diploma—who possibly should not have been licensed in the first place—to continue to practice medicine. It placed this ninety-three-year-old man on five years' probation, the only condition of which was that he inform his patients in writing that his treatments were experimental. The board offered no explanation for its decision. Today, Revici is still practicing medicine from his Park Avenue office in Manhattan. His probationary period has ended.

Revici recently was heard on a radio talk show, discussing a new treatment he had developed for AIDS. Patients are brought into his office in a coma, it was said on the show, and two days later they are healthy enough to walk out under their own power.

In many of the cases described in this book we have changed the names of the people involved, for legal reasons and to prevent possible exploitation of the victims and their families. But Emanuel Revici is this individual's real name. And we sometimes wish we could shout it from every rooftop in America. We believe that Revici and his methods pose a continuing hazard to the health and safety of countless people who have been diagnosed with cancer. We cannot miss an opportunity to inform the public about the true history of this man and to warn people against his seductive, but dangerous methods.

How could the Revici case happen? How could such an obviously incompetent individual be licensed by the state of New York—or any state—and allowed to provide treatment to cancer patients? It would be bad enough if he were seeing only patients who are hopelessly ill, for whom conventional treatment is unlikely to have any value. In those cases, one could argue—though we would disagree—that patients should be allowed to pursue whatever slender hope they choose. In fact, an associate of Revici's wrote a letter to the *Journal of the American Medical Association* (January 8, 1949), after one of its critiques of his methods, offering just that explanation: Revici's patients were all terminal, and therefore had nothing to lose even if his treatment failed. Our view and that of most health-care professionals is that, even if the odds are against a patient's surviving, it is better to take a chance with the best treatment that can be provided in the most reputable medical center available. The Revici method is useless and offers no hope even to these difficult cases.

In any event, the charges we made against Revici never had anything to do with his treatment of terminal cancer patients. Rena Menska had a walnut-size rectal tumor. Surgery was likely to have been successful, since cases like hers have a cure rate of approximately 90 percent. The Revici method caused her a year and a half of torturous pain and indignity, leading up to a senseless and preventable death.

In the Revici case the medical community took the unusual position of working against the offending physician, complaining to the state and county medical societies and to the State Health Department. Why wasn't something done?

The fact is that this case is not unusual. At least this time some effort was made by some state employees, albeit a futile one, to strip the doctor of his license. Around the country, just as in the

Revici case in New York, state medical licensing boards charged with the responsibility of revoking the licenses of incompetent physicians are neglecting their obligation to protect the public. All too often, they say, they are understaffed and overwhelmed by complaints. Either they or the elected officials above them lack the will to put the resources into an effort to crack down on doctors who maim and kill their patients.

"There has been an increase in the number of complaints and a decrease in staff to investigate and prosecute them," the chief counsel to New York's Office of Professional Conduct, which investigates complaints against doctors, told the *Daily News* in November of 1991. "It doesn't take a rocket scientist to know the public is at risk."

According to Public Citizen, a Washington, D.C.–based consumer advocacy group, information supplied by the Federation of State Medical Boards shows that New York State ranks 49th out of fifty states and the District of Columbia in the percentage of doctors it disciplines. In 1991, out of almost 61,000 physicians practicing in the state, only 54 were the subject of disciplinary action. That's 54 actions, not license revocations. Included in that number are undefined "losses of privileges," limitations or restrictions placed on doctors while they practice, actions that resulted in temporary probation, and actions that were permanently stayed— never actually imposed—by state authorities.

The federation doesn't break down its statistics to show the types of offenses that resulted in these actions, but the vast majority were probably against doctors accused of crimes other than malpractice—Medicaid fraud, overbilling, sexual abuse of patients. Only a handful had anything to do with incompetence, negligence, or malpractice.

New York State has received much criticism for its inability to protect the public from incompetent physicians—it is near the bottom of the barrel. In using New York as an example of a nationwide problem, we may be offering a slightly exaggerated picture— but only slightly. The problems in New York exist in virtually every state and illustrate the type of systems in place elsewhere.

Here's the way it's supposed to work: A patient files a complaint with the Office of Professional Medical Conduct, a branch of the State Health Department. The staff of this Office is supposed to investigate the complaint and pass on a report to a committee at the Health Department. If the committee believes that the complaint has merit, a special panel is formed consisting of two physicians and the State Health Commissioner. The panel holds hearings on the case and formulates a recommendation. If it recommends disciplinary action, the case is passed on to the State Board of Regents, which makes the final ruling.

As we've said, very few cases get this far. And even among those that do, the vast majority of recommendations for discipline are either overruled or stayed by the Board of Regents. In fact, over an eight-year period, the New York State Board of Regents allowed more than 350 doctors who had been found by the Health Department to have committed serious misconduct to continue practicing medicine. It did so through several methods, some of which can only be interpreted as duplicitous attempts to give the appearance of taking action while letting bad doctors off the hook. In 31 percent of the cases, the Regents reduced significantly the action recommended by the Health Department. In 93 percent of the cases, it utilized a maneuver called a stay, through which it imposed the sentence on paper, then "stayed" it, allowing the doctor to continue to practice and rendering the action meaningless.

"New York State regularly allows doctors to continue treating patients after ordering their licenses revoked or suspended for such serious offenses as sexual molestation, botched surgery, drug pushing and Medicaid fraud," reported Kathleen Kerr in *New York Newsday* (June 22, 1991). "Hundreds of these physicians, some of whom have been jailed for their offenses, still practice medicine because of a state discipline system that critics say is often lenient toward problem doctors."

In 1991, a New York doctor was arrested and brought up on criminal charges after destroying a fetus during an abortion performed at an unsafe and unsanitary abortion clinic on Manhattan's Lower East Side. The doctor, who advertised for patients in local newspapers, charged exorbitant fees to desperate, often underage women. The patient in question paid all the money she had—$1,500—to this doctor, then gave birth to a child whose arm had been cut off during what had apparently been a botched abortion.

When it was disclosed that numerous previous complaints had been filed with the state against this doctor over a period of three years, and that no action had been taken against him, New York's media began to investigate. What they found was that this type of horror was commonplace. On November 22, 1991, the *Daily News* reported that:

> hundreds of doctors continue to practice even though they are under investigation for medical misconduct by the state Health Department—and New Yorkers have no way of knowing who they are.
>
> With only 13 investigators to handle them, a staggering backlog of 1,500 complaints of medical negligence and incompetence has jammed the state Office of Professional Medical Conduct.
>
> Fifty of the most serious cases of malpractice involving New York City doctors languish in Albany waiting assignment to Health Department lawyers. . . .
>
> State health officials said that although investigators have ample evidence of patient harm to warrant disciplinary hearings against 300 doctors, the department has only 18 lawyers to handle the cases.
>
> All the while, New Yorkers are kept in the dark about who the dangerous doctors are.
>
> The names of doctors under investigation are kept confidential and only become part of the public record when the state issues official charges against them.
>
> Even then, the department does not publicize the names unless a newspaper or consumer specifically inquires. . . .
>
> On average complaints take two years to be resolved and in cases where doctors seek delays, their cases can clog the bureaucracy for up to a decade.

On December 9, 1991, the *News* said:

> Investigators are drowning in a staggering backlog of 2,300 complaints statewide, including 1,500 in New York City. . . . And

the complaints keep pouring in—2,848 were filed from January through October 1991.

The doctors include gynecologists, surgeons, psychiatrists and internists. Their crimes range from medical negligence and sexual abuse of patients to taking drugs on the job and practicing while psychiatrically impaired.

The fifty-four actions taken against doctors in New York State in 1991 is down from ninety-eight three years earlier—still a paltry total, but at least somewhat better. And despite its having been criticized repeatedly over the years, nothing much has changed. As long ago as 1980, a State Assembly committee charged the state agency with "poor management, unjustifiable delays and inadequate results." The committee chairman said the state was indifferent to the nature of the crisis occurring, had a "smug attitude," a "go-slow" approach, and no particular desire to change.

Unfortunately, nothing happened when the State Assembly criticized the state's performance in 1980, and even with the avalanche of publicity that followed the nightmarish abortion-clinic case in 1991, nothing has happened. The state has acted with indifference to the public health threat, with complaints languishing in its files. In fact, the state turned down an offer of free help.

Our law firm contacted the State Health Department, pointing out that the huge backlog of complaints was a public health emergency. We offered to provide our services on a *pro bono* basis to help clear away some of the cases, with the stipulation that we would not review any cases in which we had a private interest, nor would we take on clients who had complaints under consideration by the state. We were offering a life preserver to a drowning man, but it was turned down. The department said it preferred to obtain increased funds from the state budget and hire additional staff attorneys. To date, new attorneys have not been hired. Since New York is in the midst of serious budgetary problems, such a prospect seems unlikely. The complaints keep piling up at a rate of 3,000 a year, but they are just added to the mounting backlog.

Hardly any state does a good job of protecting the public from incompetent doctors. In 1991, in the entire United States, 2,013 disciplinary actions were taken against doctors by state licensing boards. A large percentage of these involved fraud and various crimes other than malpractice. And many of the actions imposed penalties that were something less than the permanent revocation of a doctor's license.

Compare those statistics to indicators of the overall malpractice epidemic. There are nearly 600,000 physicians licensed to practice medicine in this country. Authoritative estimates indicate that 60,000 to 90,000 of those physicians may be practicing medicine while impaired by drugs or alcohol; thousands are guilty of over-billing, Medicaid fraud, sexual harassment and abuse, and other crimes. One hundred thousand Americans die each year in hospitals as a result of malpractice; thousands more die uncounted in doctors' offices and free-standing clinics. Hundreds of thousands are seriously injured. Thirty thousand a year die due to misprescribed drugs; prescription errors result in the hospitalization of ten times that number of patients; as many as 24,000 patients lose their lives due to medical errors during unnecessary operations. Compared to those statistics, 2,013 disciplinary actions, only a fraction of which were meaningful actions against negligent physicians, is disgraceful.

The Public Citizen Health Research Group's annual ranking of states' effectiveness in disciplining doctors is based on information gathered by the Federation of State Medical Boards. Critics would argue that these statistics don't tell you much because they simply compare the number of serious disciplinary actions with the total number of doctors licensed to practice in a particular state. Theoretically, a state could be doing a good job of enforcement, but still get a low rating for disciplining a small number of doctors—if there are fewer bad doctors in that state than in other states to begin with. However, there is no evidence that this contention is valid. There is no reason why doctors in one state should be any more or less competent than doctors in another state. If all states have approximately the same percentage of good and bad physicians—which should logically be the case—then the differences in the rate of disciplinary action can only relate to the effectiveness of each state's efforts.

As Public Citizen points out:

> The disparity between states with higher rates of doctor disci-
> pline and states with only a fraction of those rates is cause
> for alarm by the residents of the low-discipline states. People
> in these states are much more likely than people in high-
> discipline states to be injured or killed by doctors still on the
> loose because they haven't been "caught." What would be
> unacceptable medical practice in one state may go unnoticed
> by the state licensing board in another state.

Following is Public Citizen's state-by-state rankings for 1991, list-
ing the best states first:

State	Number of Actions	Total Number of Doctors	Actions per 1,000 Doctors
Alaska	14	777	18.02
Oklahoma	89	5,095	17.47
Iowa	55	4,728	11.63
Georgia	115	11,929	9.64
Kentucky	64	6,701	9.55
Mississippi	34	3,753	9.06
Louisiana	65	8,689	7.48
W. Virginia	24	3,388	7.08
Wyoming	5	734	6.81
Vermont	11	1,631	6.74
S. Carolina	41	6,096	6.73
Missouri	66	10,759	6.13
N. Dakota	7	1,195	5.86
Oregon	37	6,562	5.64
Indiana	53	9,558	5.55
Delaware	8	1,449	5.52
Colorado	38	7,606	5.00
Utah	17	3,406	4.99
Montana	7	1,452	4.82
New Jersey	92	20,579	4.47
Texas	135	31,647	4.27
Arizona	34	8,226	4.13
Ohio	94	23,239	4.04

(continued)

State	Number of Actions	Total Number of Doctors	Actions per 1,000 Doctors
Washington	45	11,325	3.97
Kansas	18	4,861	3.70
Nevada	7	1,921	3.64
Florida	114	31,483	3.62
Minnesota	35	10,458	3.35
Arkansas	13	3,966	3.28
Connecticut	35	10,699	3.27
Alabama	21	6,964	3.02
Virginia	41	13,795	2.97
New Mexico	9	3,114	2.89
Idaho	4	1,435	2.79
Wisconsin	28	10,049	2.79
Illinois	73	26,603	2.74
California	204	78,285	2.61
Tennessee	26	10,334	2.52
Nebraska	7	2,955	2.37
Michigan	44	18,620	2.36
Hawaii	6	2,809	2.14
Maryland	31	16,716	1.85
N. Carolina	25	13,492	1.85
New Hampshire	4	2,507	1.60
D. of Columbia	6	3,929	1.53
Maine	3	2,522	1.19
Pennsylvania	33	30,824	1.07
Massachusetts	22	21,475	1.02
New York	54	60,744	0.89
South Dakota	0	1,093	0.00
Rhode Island	0	2,744	0.00
Total	2,013	584,921	3.44

As you can see, the results cut across geographic region and state size. West Virginia is in the top ten, while Rhode Island—a state with close to the same number of physicians—is last. The discipline rate in Texas is about twice that in California, and New Jersey takes five times as many actions per doctor as New York. Are there more bad doctors in New Jersey than in New York? More bad doctors in West Virginia than in Rhode Island? Of course not. Authorities in some states are more stringent than in others; and there is no doubt that lives are saved as a result.

With few exceptions, virtually no state does anything close to the type of job it should. That only 2,013 disciplinary actions of any kind were taken nationwide is appalling, not only by our standards but even by those of the malpractice insurance companies that usually protect these offending physicians.

Obviously, negligent doctors get sued more often than generally competent ones. Therefore, it is against the interests of these insurance companies to carry policies on doctors who are frequent subjects of litigation. In 1989, according to a Tufts University study, malpractice insurance companies either terminated coverage or placed restrictions on the practices of more than 7,700 physicians whose performance they viewed as substandard or prone to negligence. That's compared to 2,013 disciplinary actions by states. Even these insurance companies, usually advocates for physicians, found almost four times as many physicians prone to negligence as did state licensing boards.

Unfortunately, as a general rule states make no effort to follow up on actions taken by insurance companies. One would think that if an insurance company cancelled a doctor's policy because they believe he is prone to negligence, the state licensing board might want to investigate. But that just doesn't happen.

In fact, even when a physician's malpractice insurance is cancelled, there is no restriction against him or her practicing medicine. Although drivers in many states are required to purchase liability insurance before they can register their cars, there is no such requirement for doctors. And uninsured doctors can mean trouble for patients. If a doctor commits malpractice and has no insurance, the patient may have little or no recourse. Even if a case against such a doctor goes to trial and the patient receives a large judgment, there is often no way of collecting it. Of course, whatever assets the physician has can be attached, but what if he or she claims to have no assets? It can take years of wrangling to obtain the funds, if any can be obtained at all.

If bureaucrats were serious about cracking down on malpractice, they could do so with a simple step. It would require no additional manpower or resources. They could let private insurance companies do their legwork for them. States should require physicians to obtain malpractice insurance in order to maintain their license. Require physicians to show proof of their insurance policy to the state when they apply for a license, and require insurance companies to report to the state any policies they terminate or place restrictions on. States could improve their enforcement efforts overnight by at least four times. And possibly, we could reduce a large percentage of the malpractice that is taking place in America today.

Lest we give the impression that we are tarring all state licensing boards, we must point out that even those states that do a relatively good job don't do anywhere near as good a job as they should. Even the states that rank relatively high often have a sad record. The state of Indiana, for example, ranks fifteenth according to Public Citizen, imposing about six times as many disciplinary actions per physician as does New York. But according to a Pulitzer Prize–winning investigation by the *Indianapolis Star* that appeared in June 1990, even in that state,

> Nothing has been done to stop a handful of doctors who have committed malpractice again and again. While the doctors go undisciplined, their patients suffer disabling injuries, disfigurement—even death. . . .
>
> A handful of Indiana doctors have maimed and mutilated scores of patients in this state and nothing has been done to stop them. They have not lost their licenses. They have not lost their hospital privileges. They have not, in many cases, even paid more for malpractice insurance.
>
> Instead of rooting out physicians who repeatedly cause malpractice, the state has created a system that, in effect, protects them. . . . No matter how many times a doctor commits malpractice, he is not likely to lose his medical license in Indiana unless he commits a crime, abuses drugs or is disciplined first in another state.

The Indiana system is not dissimilar from others around the country. Complaints of misconduct are filed with the state attorney general's office, which usually asks a member of the state medical licensing board for an initial evaluation. The attorney general's office conducts an investigation, and if it feels the case has merit, it can file charges with the licensing board. The board can hold hearings and impose whatever disciplinary actions it deems appropriate.

But like most medical licensing boards, Indiana's is not protecting the public from even the worst offenders. The few doctors it does punish are rarely the ones who are committing the most malpractice. Approximately 84 percent of the doctors against whom sanctions were imposed were found to have been drug abusers, criminals, or individuals who had already been disciplined in other states. Only a small fraction had anything to do with negligence or incompetent medical practice.

As elsewhere, in Indiana the public is kept in the dark about negligent doctors. And the general public is not the only party who is ill-informed. Eight local hospitals employed physicians who had had at least three successful malpractice lawsuits against them with awards in excess of $100,000. When asked, each hospital said it would be concerned about having doctors with three such awards against them on its staff. Yet apparently none of the hospitals was aware that it was doing just that. In fact, one hospital used two of these repeat offenders in its advertising campaign, promoting them in ads headlined: "How to recognize a good physician when you see one." The hospitals obviously were unable to recognize bad physicians when they saw them, despite Indiana laws requiring that awards over $100,000 in malpractice cases be reported to the State Insurance Department.

The people of Indiana, along with citizens in New York, California, and elsewhere around the United States, may soon begin to realize that what we need is not legal reform but medical reform. Twenty-seven thousand deaths and injuries in one year in New York hospitals documented to have been caused by negligence, yet between 1986 and 1991 the state disciplined between 54 and 167 doctors a year. Twenty-four thousand deaths and injuries in one year in California hospitals documented to have been caused by malpractice, yet between 1986 and 1991 that state took action against between 93 and 204 doctors a year.

While a few states seem to be trying to weed out incompetent doctors, the vast majority make only a negligible effort. To its credit, New York commissioned one of the most comprehensive studies of this issue ever conducted—the much-quoted Harvard study discussed in chapter 1. But even this study had serious limitations. The Harvard team based its investigation on cases for which the statute of limitations on legal action had expired. Therefore, none of the negligent doctors examined in the study can be sued for malpractice. The cases described are anonymous, so that the public will never know the identity of the physicians involved.

State officials failed to compile the names of those doctors the researchers determined had committed malpractice. Had they done even that much, investigators could have followed up, reviewing other cases in which they had been involved and determining whether the negligence followed a pattern. Unless we put systems into place that work on behalf of the public, the malpractice crisis is not going to abate.

There are several steps that need to be taken. States should not be allowed to hide beneath the cloak of fiscal austerity to explain their inability to discipline doctors in prompt fashion. It is not a matter of money, it is a matter of will. It would be a simple matter, as we've said, to require doctors to have insurance and to require insurance companies to inform authorities any time they restrict or terminate a physician's policy. By taking even that small step, we could improve public safety dramatically.

Besides, taxpayers are paying the cost of all the malpractice that these physicians are guilty of. It's the cost of a lifetime of medical care for disabled children, of surgery to repair damage resulting from negligently performed procedures, of unnecessary operations, of misprescribed drugs. Malpractice costs a lot of money. Identifying incompetent physicians, stripping them of their licenses, and alerting the public to their offenses would cost a fraction of that amount.

Obviously, money is not the real issue. Medical licensing boards and peer review organizations are usually dominated by physicians, who are inclined to give a fellow doctor a break. If these boards are to be effective, they must be restructured to represent the public interest fairly and aggressively. Of course, it is important to have the medical community represented, to have the benefit of a doctor's point of view and expertise on complicated medical matters. However, these boards should include greater numbers of public members from all walks of life—people who have distinguished themselves in terms of intelligence, diligence, and public service.

Finally, the process of medical reform should be open to the public. Patients should be able to determine easily whether the doctor who is treating them is capable or is someone with a record of abusing and neglecting patients. State licensing boards should publicize their proceedings and their results.

Congress has an important role to play in this process as well. In 1986, it passed legislation creating a national directory of physicians who have been found liable for malpractice or against whom disciplinary actions have been imposed. It also includes those doctors who have been sued, whose cases never made it to court because they agreed prior to trial to settle and pay the patients. This data bank got off to a rocky start, but if it functions properly, it will be the first and only centralized directory providing this critical information. That's the good news.

The bad news is that the data bank is not open to the public. The information exists, but the people who need it can't have it. If Congress is serious about protecting its constituents, it will ensure that this data bank makes accessible information consumers need.

Also, the federal government's Health Care Financing Agency (HCFA) regularly and with much fanfare compiles and releases the mortality rates at hospitals around the country. Presumably, this information is offered to let the public know which hospitals in their communities they would be most likely to die in. Hospitals argue, however, that these statistics do no such thing. And the government agrees. The statistics, they say, do not take into account mitigating factors such as the age of the patient population, the seriousness of the illnesses, or whether some hospitals admit a large number of terminal cancer or AIDS patients. As a result, any hospital that receives a low rating regularly argues that there are mitigating factors, limiting the survey's usefulness.

If it is going to expend its resources in this way, the government should go one small step further. As it compiles these mortality statistics, its investigators should take some extra time and evaluate the cause of death. Was the death unavoidable or was it negligence? Did the hospital admit a larger than usual number of elderly patients, or were most of the deaths the result of elective surgery? As long as HCFA is going through this process, why not make it more meaningful? Why not conduct a survey that gives information we can use?

Also, the Food and Drug Administration must take on the job of policing drug advertisements in medical journals. As we discussed earlier, neither the journals, which rely on these ads for revenue, nor the manufacturers, which are trying to peddle a product, can be trusted with the responsibility of ensuring accuracy. The FDA must do it and, if it lacks the resources, it should charge drug companies for the new expense. Require the manufacturers to submit all their proposed ads to the FDA before they are published, together with documentation of their veracity and an appropriate administrative fee to cover the FDA's costs. A wide range of government agencies routinely charge filing fees for such applications. This would be a much-needed extension of that policy and would, at no cost to the government, provide an added measure of protection to the public.

Finally, if state governments refuse to protect the public from inadequate or incompetent medical care, then the federal government must do it. If Congress can investigate ethical lapses in government, appoint special counsels to probe for sources of leaks to the news media, it can certainly investigate the reprehensible practices that take place in medicine.

If the states won't act appropriately, the federal government should take over the function of licensing and disciplining doctors. Apart from the appalling lack of discipline imposed anywhere, there is no reason why standards should vary from state to state, why one state should do a better job of enforcement than another. Standards of medical care are virtually the same across the country, and patients everywhere should be entitled to a uniform quality of care. Or if not uniform quality, they should at least have the assurance that they will be uniformly protected from the worst the medical profession has to offer, no matter where they live.

5

YOU COULDN'T HAVE KNOWN

When politicians talk about recidivists, they usually mean muggers and other violent criminals who commit crimes repeatedly. Most of these criminals—at least at some point in their careers—wind up in jail. When criminals prey on innocent victims, public officials talk tough, the public rallies around their calls for public safety, and government resources are marshaled to meet the threat. Allowing repeat offenders to stay on the street is grossly unacceptable to most responsible citizens. Imagine the public outcry there would be if it came to light that one of these criminals was maiming or killing people continually over a period of years. Imagine the fury we would all feel if it turned out that the person were allowed to continue perpetrating these crimes while public officials did nothing to stop him.

Well, it happens all the time. Rather than Son of Sam or Charles Manson, the perpetrators we're talking about are physicians who commit malpractice again and again, and are allowed to continue to practice medicine, undeterred by colleagues who know of their actions.

The Principles of Medical Ethics of the American Medical Association states: "The medical profession should safeguard the public and itself against physicians deficient in moral character or professional competence. Physicians should observe all laws, uphold the dignity and honor of the profession and accept its self-imposed disciplines. They should expose, without hesitation, illegal or unethical conduct of fellow members of the profession."

Worthwhile, noble principles. Unfortunately, according to Dr. Malcolm C. Todd, a past president of the AMA, "Physicians often hesitate to be too critical of another doctor, because they fear it will get them in trouble with their colleagues and they'd lose referral work. We recognize this as a weakness, and we are trying to make amends. Another reason is that malpractice suits might get [filed], and doctors basically don't like to go to court [to testify against other doctors]. . . ."

That's the reality. Doctors don't report misconduct and they don't like to testify against other doctors, either formally or informally. Physicians are closest to the scene of the crime. They are most likely to have knowledge of incidents of malpractice. They almost always know the identity of the bad doctors among them. Yet they rarely disclose this information and are extremely unlikely to file complaints with local medical societies or state licensing boards. Even the courts have made note of what one judicial decision called "a shocking unethical reluctance on the part of the medical profession to accept its obligation to society and its profession in an action for malpractice" (*Steiginga* v. *Thron*, 1954).

Physicians and medical societies say it's not their job to identify and crack down on bad doctors—that it's up to the states. But clearly the states are not doing it. And one of the reasons state authorities do such a bad job is that physicians rarely provide the information they require. Several years ago, we learned that in New York, for example, of 1,700 complaints that had been filed against doctors with the State Office of Professional Medical Conduct during a one-year period, only five had come from any of the sixty-two county medical societies.

As with so many issues surrounding the malpractice debate, the conspiracy of silence is nothing new. It goes back to the early days of malpractice litigation. In 1842, the Cortland County, New York, Medical Society, an outspoken critic of lawyers and lawsuits, attempted to enact formal rules prohibiting doctors from investigating the actions of other doctors. An outraged medical journal of the time wrote: "They create among the public an impression that physicians are disposed to screen each other from the just consequences of ignorance and incapacity, that they regard their duty to their patients as secondary, and that, as in the present instance, they deem the preservation of limb and life as of little weight in the balance with the observance of a false code of professional etiquette."

This philosophy was no less evident when Dr. William Nolen wrote in his 1972 book, *Surgeon's World:*

> We doctors reserve for ourselves the right to decide what is and is not within our range of competence. Even if everyone else on the staff agreed with me that Jack shouldn't do major surgery, no one would side with me if I were to try and prevent him from operating. He has an M.D., a license to practice medicine and surgery, and I have no right to interfere with that license unless I can prove gross negligence, which I can't. If I were to ax Jack Nadler, my confreres would ask themselves, Which one of us might be next? Doctors make a show of policing themselves but in fact don't do much of a job of it. . . .
>
> We're too afraid of hurting the feelings of our confreres, of losing referrals from them, of being overcritical. We lean over backward in order not to judge our fellow-doctors too harshly, and often we do this to such an extreme that it poses a threat to the well-being of patients. A surgeon practically has to become a mass murderer before his fellow surgeons will take away his surgical privileges.

Dr. James Burt apparently did not quite meet that standard. A non–board-certified general surgeon, Dr. Burt began his obstetrics and gynecology practice at St. Elizabeth Medical Center in Dayton, Ohio, in 1951 and built a successful practice there, eventually seeing thousands of patients at his office in the hospital. In the decades that followed, Dr. Burt engaged in practices that mutilated thousands of women. The Burt case is one of the most bizarre we have ever encountered, and while for the purposes of this book we have altered the names of the patients he victimized, the names of this physician, James Burt, and of the hospital where he practiced, are accurate. (The names of other doctors in this chapter have also been changed.)

In the course of his practice, Dr. Burt dreamt up a new type of surgical procedure that he apparently believed would enhance women's enjoyment of sexual intercourse. It seemed to Dr. Burt that the normal female anatomy was not arranged in a way that allowed for optimal sexual pleasure and, therefore, he devised a technique to construct an artificial extension of the vagina, tighten and reposition the vaginal opening, and "circumcise" the clitoris.

In 1973, Kim Harrigan and her husband, Ed, met Dr. Burt for the first time. She was pregnant with their first child, and a friend had given her Dr. Burt's name. St. Elizabeth was the hospital in the community that they had always used, and it seemed a convenient, logical choice.

The pregnancy proceeded normally as Mr. and Mrs. Harrigan took Lamaze classes together and awaited the birth of their child. They went together to all of her doctor's appointments and, although the dim lights in the examining room prevented Mr. Harrigan from seeing what was going on, they both always went home reassured that both baby and mother were healthy and well.

When she went into labor, they called Dr. Burt immediately and he met them at the hospital and rushed the expectant mother into a delivery room. Mr. Harrigan began to follow, expecting to be present for the delivery as planned, but the doctor stopped him at the door and asked him to remain outside. The father-to-be was concerned, he paced around the waiting area, but he assumed that everything was under control.

During the pregnancy Dr. Burt had prescribed various medications to relax the patient and relieve whatever discomfort she was experiencing. While she was giving birth, he medicated her further, rendering her virtually unconscious. After what seemed like a relatively normal labor, she gave birth to a healthy baby boy.

In the recovery room later on, Ms. Harrigan complained of tightness in the vaginal area, saying that she felt as though she'd been sewed up. Dr. Burt told her, "Honey, you were big—a Mack truck could have fit in you." He told her she needed to relax and that she would thank him later. He then made a circle with his fingers and asked her if her husband was "bigger than that."

When Ms. Harrigan got home, she began to experience serious health problems. She contracted bladder infections and yeast infections approximately every two months. She was unable to control her urine and had to wipe herself constantly. She would wake up in the middle of the night with pain in her rectal area. She had a constant burning and itching sensation, and intercourse, when she and her husband tried it at all, was extremely painful. She knew something was wrong, but she did not know what. She knew that she felt differently, but could not tell exactly what had happened to her.

Without her knowledge, Dr. Burt had circumcised her, tightened her vaginal walls, and created a pouchlike flap in front of her vagina.

That same year, Lee Ann Johnson also visited Dr. Burt at his office at St. Elizabeth. This twenty-three-year-old woman had been living with her boyfriend for some time. They were in love and trying, without success, to have a child. Ms. Johnson asked Dr. Burt if he could determine whether there was some reason why she had not become pregnant and whether he could correct it.

Dr. Burt told her that she would need to have some tests done to determine the nature of the problem. He injected a dye into her bloodstream and took several X-rays, saying that this test was to see if she was pregnant. He turned down the lights in the examining room and told her to remove her clothes so that he could examine her breasts. She complied. When he finished with her breasts, he turned the lights back up and moved on to an examination of her vagina, during which she felt his face pressing up against her pubic area.

Finally, Dr. Burt pronounced his diagnosis: surgery would indeed solve her problem. First he would do a D&C. Then, according to Ms. Johnson, he said he was going to operate to "lift something up inside her so that the sperm would go directly in." He told her that she needed to relax more and that after this surgery, she would be able to get pregnant. A week later, she was admitted to St. Elizabeth and the surgery was performed.

Immediately following the operation—virtually as soon as she came out of the anesthesia—Ms. Johnson began to experience pain, which became excruciating as the hours passed. Dr. Burt told her to relax, that she'd be fine. He brought her boyfriend into her hospital room and proceeded to demonstrate with his fingers how they would have to have sex. He told them that Ms. Johnson would be like a virgin now, that her opening would be tight, that it might hurt her a little at first. If intercourse proved difficult, he told them, they should practice anal or oral sex for the time being.

Despite Dr. Burt's explanation, the pain never abated, but became a constant part of Lee Ann Johnson's life. In order to urinate, she had to lean forward at a certain angle; otherwise, the urine would collect in pockets of flesh that now existed over her vagina and rectum. It was impossible to keep herself clean. She had to wear a sanitary pad at all times and contracted repeated infections.

About a month after her surgery she ended her relationship with Dr. Burt and began seeing a succession of other physicians in the community, in the hope that someone would be able to do something to help her. One of the doctors she saw—about four years later—was Dr. Sam Alafah, who immediately recognized what had been done and asked her about her surgery. After hearing her history, Dr. Alafah called in several of his colleagues to examine her. He wanted them to see what he called the "surgery of love."

In 1984, eleven years after Dr. Burt promised that his surgery would allow her to conceive a child, she finally did get pregnant. She suffered a miscarriage, however. At that time, she was under the care of Dr. Peter Poole, who, during his first examination of her, said: "Dr. Burt got hold of you, didn't he?" When she pressed him to discuss Burt's surgery further, he refused.

In 1987, Ms. Johnson finally had the child she wanted, a son, delivered by cesarean section. Her obstetrician at the time discovered seven fibroid tumors in her uterus, which he removed. He also told her that her bladder was torn—her legacy from Dr. Burt—which required him to catheterize her for three weeks. Today, her numerous sanitary and health problems remain. Sexual intercourse became so painful that she and her boyfriend eventually stopped trying completely. They remain devoted to each other, but now sleep in separate bedrooms.

That day in Dr. Alafah's office in 1977 was the first time Ms. Johnson had heard the term "surgery of love." However, since 1975, Dr. Burt had received widespread attention as a result of a book he had written by that same name. In *Surgery of Love,* which he paid a vanity press to publish, and which had an illustration on its cover of a scalpel with little red hearts trailing off it, Burt described the nature of his surgery and claimed to have improved the sex lives of hundreds of women. He admitted that he was performing this surgery without the knowledge or consent of his patients, while they were under sedation during deliveries or undergoing other surgical procedures that they had consented to. He said in this book that he had been performing the surgery for years—that in fact he had performed it on his own wife—and that his procedure was well known within the local medical community.

Indeed, Dr. Burt's love surgery must have been very well known at St. Elizabeth Medical Center. A physician does not perform surgery alone—a team of doctors and nurses is always present. His colleagues on the staff of the hospital clearly were aware of this practice. If they were not, the publication of his book, and Dr. Burt's subsequent publicity appearances on local talk shows and in newspapers, must have alerted them.

The matter obviously concerned the medical community somewhat. The local medical society asked the dean of the State University Medical School to review the scientific claims in Dr. Burt's book. The dean's reply was that the book was "poorly written, medically unfounded, and [that] a rebuttal to the author would only add dignity to its existence."

Did the medical society take any action to stop Dr. Burt? No. Did it take any steps to warn the public of the risks associated with this procedure? No. Rather, Dr. Burt became a dirty joke among physicians in the community, who made demeaning, tittering comments like "Dr. Burt got ahold of you, didn't he?" to their patients.

One past president of the county medical society was quoted later as saying, "Everybody knew that he had this obsession with probing women's sex lives, but most people smiled about it." Another past president of the society said, "Doctors tended to ignore it, or to feel embarrassed by it."

St. Elizabeth was a well-respected institution in the community. The hospital had a reputation for quality and had the trust of its patients. It embued all of its physicians, including Dr. Burt, with that aura of respectability. The guidelines for hospital accreditation that St. Elizabeth was bound to uphold required it to supervise its staff and all medical and surgical procedures performed there, to ensure that only approved surgical procedures were performed and only with the informed consent of each patient.

Despite the clear fact that Dr. Burt was performing this bizarre surgery on thousands of patients for many years, admittedly without their consent and causing them serious physical harm, neither St. Elizabeth nor the county medical society took any steps to stop him. Even after publication of his book, when Burt was quoted in the local newspaper openly extolling the virtues of his procedure and claiming that "almost 100 percent of the women operated on have been as ecstatic over the results as his own wife," no one felt the need to warn the public. No one felt obliged to stop Dr. Burt from routinely butchering unsuspecting women.

In 1978, after discreet inquiries by the medical society, St. Elizabeth asked Dr. Burt to provide a detailed written explanation of the "surgery of love" to the hospital executive committee, which he gladly did. Several months later, after reviewing the doctor's work, the hospital decided to require him, in all future cases, to obtain a special consent form from his patients stating his procedure as "an unproven, nonstandard practice of gynecology." In taking this action, St. Elizabeth was virtually admitting that this substandard practice had been taking place under its roof for years. But it did nothing to notify past, current, or future patients, did nothing publicly to discredit Dr. Burt or his surgery, and did nothing to prevent him from continuing to indulge his obscene obsession.

In 1980, Jane Lippitt, a thirty-four-year-old, happily married mother of three children, went to see Dr. Burt at St. Elizabeth, complaining of severe abdominal cramps, lower back pain, and occasional spotting between periods. He performed a cursory examination and informed the patient that she needed a total hysterectomy. She asked him to explain the surgery, why it was needed, what exactly would be done, and how she would feel afterward, but he refused. It would be impossible, Dr. Burt told her, for a layperson to understand such a complicated procedure. That, he said, was why he went to medical school.

Ms. Lippitt went home and thought about it, and decided that she was probably worried about nothing. Dr. Burt was a doctor, after all, practicing at a trusted institution, and he did seem to know what he was doing. So a short time later, she went ahead with the surgery. During her last visit to the doctor's office prior to the surgery, he presented her with a stack of forms to sign. When she asked what they were, he told her that they were just some standard forms the hospital required for the surgery.

When she returned home after her eleven-day hospital stay, Ms. Lippett almost immediately began to feel the effects of Dr. Burt's work. She felt pain and discomfort, had difficulty urinating, and contracted a succession of severe infections. When she finally went to see another gynecologist a few months later, the doctor examined her, recognized the love surgery, and told her that Dr. Burt had circumcised her and "moved things around." This female gynecologist told Ms. Lippitt that, as with the earlier cases we described, urine was collecting inside her vagina and causing her infections. She advised her to purchase surgical gloves and stretch out her vaginal area when she urinated.

Ms. Lippett eventually lost sensation in her bladder and no longer had the ability to tell when she needed to urinate. At times she urinates without realizing it; other times, her bladder fills up—causing a great deal of pain—and she cannot urinate. On those occasions she must insert a catheter to allow the urine to drain. Her normal practice now is to urinate every two hours or so to make sure that the urine is not building up in her bladder without her knowledge. But recently, during a Christmastime trip to the mall, she suddenly experienced the pain that comes when her bladder expands unexpectedly. She made her way to the ladies room, slumped down on the filthy floor, and couldn't get up. She had no choice but to insert a catheter right there, and since she had nothing in which to collect the urine, it drained onto the bathroom floor. When she recovered, she found a mop and suffered the further indignity of having to clean up the mess.

Today Ms. Lippitt's life is in a shambles. She continues to have frequent infections of her bladder, kidney, and vagina. She has scar tissue up through her colon and has no wall left between her vagina and rectum.

Unable to engage in intercourse or other day-to-day activities, her marriage began to suffer and she was eventually divorced. She must keep extra clothes in the car in case of "accidents," and is afraid to go on trips or take her children camping or to the zoo, for fear of embarrassing herself. She says that she has not had a good night's sleep since Dr. Burt performed his surgery on her—that she just lies awake in her bed on top of an uncomfortable rubber mat.

Shortly after he performed surgery on Ms. Lippitt, Dr. Burt was appointed by the hospital administration to serve on its quality assurance committee, a position he held for the next four years. Rather than blow the whistle on him, this respected health-care institution—a Catholic hospital which would not allow abortions to be performed on the premises—lent him additional credibility and a facility in which to perform this bizarre surgery.

In 1988, after years of malpractice and contempt for his patients, things began to unravel for Dr. Burt. Several of his former patients filed lawsuits, and a short time later the local attorneys handling the case asked us to become involved. As the lawsuits moved forward, the local and national media picked up on the story. Gradually the public began to learn the story of what had been transpiring at St. Elizabeth Medical Center for the past twenty years. When the "love doctor" was finally dragged out and put under the light of public scrutiny, his former patients came forward in droves. Hundreds of lawsuits have now been filed, including more than forty by our office alone.

In December 1988, faced with a storm of local and national publicity, an avalanche of complaints from former patients, and an outraged public, the state licensing board finally filed charges against Dr. Burt: forty-one counts of gross negligence and gross dishonesty. It was at last seeking to punish him for acts that had been well known in the local medical community for more than twenty years. In 1989, Dr. Burt surrendered his license to practice medicine and retired to Florida, agreeing never to practice in the United States again. He obtained a license to sell real estate in Florida, but it was revoked shortly thereafter when the state found that he had lied on his application.

Faced with numerous lawsuits and potential financial liability, Dr. Burt attempted to file for personal bankruptcy, but his application was denied by the court when it was learned that he had misappropriated funds. In 1991, the first of our lawsuits against Dr. Burt—Jane Lippitt's—came to trial. The verdict: $5 million against Dr. Burt.

We also sued the hospital, charging that since it had obviously known about Dr. Burt's practices, and since these operations were clearly beyond the bounds of normal medical practice, it should have stepped in and stopped him. At the very least, St. Elizabeth should not have allowed him to practice under its roof.

Hospitals routinely perform "peer reviews," a process through which physicians at the hospital assess the performance of their fellow physicians. St. Elizabeth performed these reviews on Dr. Burt periodically, as it did on other doctors and the hospital noted its awareness of his appalling practices. But it did nothing to stop him. That, we argued, was negligent peer review.

Rather than acknowledging its failings, St. Elizabeth fought us tooth and nail, arguing up to the Supreme Court of Ohio (the state's highest appeals court) that if its peer review process *was* negligent, the negligence had occurred years in the past and that state's statute of limitations had expired. This posed a legal issue of major consequence not only to our case, but to the people of this country. It involved the basic question of a hospital's responsibility to protect the public from incompetent or impaired physicians.

The peer review process at hospitals is virtually always kept confidential, as it was at St. Elizabeth. Hospitals do not disclose their findings about doctors to their patients, the public, or any other body. Therefore, it's almost impossible for victims of malpractice to find out, until long after the malpractice has occurred, what the negligent physician's peers in the hospital had known and what— if anything—they did about it. In most cases, the statute of limitations would have expired before a lawsuit against a hospital could be filed—effectively insulating the hospital from liability.

But in a landmark decision, the court in this case ruled that the plaintiffs did not have any reason to know about the hospital's possible negligence until an exposé of the case was broadcast on TV. The statute of limitations, said the court, "commences to run when the victim knows or should have discovered that he or she was injured as a result of the hospital's negligent credentialing procedures or practices."

Because of this ruling, hospitals can be held liable—at least in Ohio and perhaps across the country if other courts follow this precedent—based on a statute of limitations that does not begin until the victim becomes aware that the hospital's peer review process may have been negligent. This ruling places more pressure on hospitals to take their peer reviews more seriously—to take meaningful action to protect their patients from doctors who are incompetent. And it sends a signal that if hospitals don't, the courts may begin to hold them legally and financially liable.

Proving the hospital's responsibility in court was important to us for another reason as well. Dr. Burt had filed for bankruptcy and claimed to be indigent and unable to pay any legal judgments against him. Even though his personal negligence is obvious and he can be held legally liable for compensating those of his victims who are successful in court, as a practical matter it is unlikely that anyone will actually be able to collect these judgments. Demonstrating St. Elizabeth's legal liability also allows us to hold it financially liable to the women who were maimed at the hospital.

As the court said in its decision: "Perhaps now [Dr. Burt's victims], and others, will have their day in court where the conspiracy of silence in the local medical community which permitted these atrocities to be committed—and the atrocities themselves— can be more fully explored."

The point of the Burt case is that, were it not for the lawsuits filed against him, were it not for the media coverage that followed those lawsuits, he would probably still be practicing medicine. Colleagues in the medical profession were aware of his practice, the medical society was aware of it, the dean of the local medical school was aware of it, and the hospital staff and administration were aware of it. They all knew that he was performing surgery without the informed consent of his patients. They all knew that he was destroying people's lives. Many of them saw firsthand what his former patients were going through, but they did nothing to stop him. They talked about him among themselves, but no one talked to the patients. They allowed him to promote a book and publicize a procedure they knew was a fraud, but they did nothing to correct the widespread misimpression he'd created. In short, they did nothing to protect the public.

Unfortunately, although the specifics of the Burt case are quite bizarre, the inability or unwillingness of the medical profession to police itself is common. While their professional organizations rail against lawyers and lawsuits, most physicians have personal knowledge of colleagues whom they view as incompetent or negligent, whom they believe may have committed malpractice. They may try to steer clear of these individuals, but do they blow the whistle on them? Rarely. When doctors do complain about other doctors, it is usually to their local medical society, which simply logs the complaint and passes the buck, saying that it's not its job to discipline bad doctors.

According to the *New York Times* (January 29, 1976),

Although incidents of careless and incompetent medical treatment are known to almost every physician, officials of medical societies and state licensing agencies say that relatively few doctors ever report them to the appropriate regulatory body.

This traditional reluctance of physicians to criticize their errant colleagues, these officials say, is perhaps the greatest obstacle to better regulation of the medical profession.

What about the AMA's principles to "safeguard the public . . . against physicians deficient in moral character or professional competence?" The medical community—with the exception of some doctors who truly do view public service as their top priority—allows incompetent physicians to commit malpractice over and over. Among hospital administrations, even when they determine that they must take action against one of their physicians, the action taken is usually nothing more than a slap on the wrist. Often, the unscrupulous practitioner is asked to resign from the hospital staff, with the understanding that no further action will be taken. It is all done in polite, genteel fashion— the hospital and physician are both spared embarrassment. And no one worries about the patients who have been mistreated. The offending doctor moves to another community or another state and sets up a new practice, with privileges at a new hospital. If someone contacts the first hospital seeking references, he or she is told that the physician resigned in good standing. No need to trouble future patients with any information about past misconduct.

Hospitals just don't like to take overt action against physicians, no matter how bad they are. The *New York Times'* article also cited an example of a New Mexico surgeon whose malpractice resulted in the death of a patient when he tied off the wrong duct during gall bladder surgery. His mistake was turned up during the autopsy and the hospital knew about it, but did nothing. A few months later, the same surgeon performed the same surgery on another patient and made exactly the same mistake. Another patient died needlessly. The hospital did nothing. It didn't inform the patient's family. It didn't stop the doctor from operating on others. It didn't even try to educate this physician about the nature of his mistake and how to prevent it in the future. It simply closed its eyes to the problem until, a few months later, it happened again. Three patients in six months, all undergoing routine surgery, died because of one doctor's ineptitude and the negligent inaction of his colleagues. Finally, after the third death, the physician in question was reported to the state licensing board, and after several weeks of investigation his license to practice medicine was revoked.

In a California case, *Gonzalez* v. *Nork,* the defendant, Dr. Nork, had been making a healthy living over a period of nine years, by performing unnecessary surgery on his patients—and performing it badly. When the judge reviewed the doctor's record during his trial, he repeatedly made references to other physicians protecting Dr. Nork and concealing evidence of his repeated malpractice.

In the case of *Rosner* v. *Eden Township Hospital District,* a doctor who was denied membership on a hospital staff on the grounds of "temperamental insuitability" sued to overturn the hospital's decision. In ruling in the doctor's favor, the court found that the hospital's determination that he was unsuitable was caused, not by a review of his qualifications, but by the part he played in testifying against another physician in a malpractice lawsuit.

And some years ago, a registered nurse from Rockland County, New York, made headlines when she testified before a State Assembly hearing that she was dismissed from her job and blackballed by other hospitals in the county. Her crime? She had voiced objections to the hospital management when another nurse unplugged patients' call buttons so that she would not be disturbed while filling out diet slips. A patient died, apparently with his hand clutching his nonfunctioning call button while the nurse had gone about her paperwork.

One of the most appalling forms of behavior in which a member of the medical profession can engage cannot be managed without the acquiescence of one's colleagues. Physicians practicing while under the influence of drugs or alcohol are placing the lives of their patients at risk. Yet under the roofs of some of the nation's best medical centers, doctors—often with the knowledge of their peers—are dealing with patients while impaired by controlled substances.

It was shocking to participate in a national television program with a panel of doctors and nurses who were recovering alcoholics or drug addicts. These individuals, who deserve at least some credit for having the courage to turn their lives around, nevertheless admitted openly to having treated patients—sometimes for years—while they were seriously impaired. They described administering medication, performing complicated tests, and generally trying to keep up with the normal hospital routine. And it was never necessary for them to keep their conditions secret. They assume in retrospect that their fellow doctors and nurses were aware of their "problem," but did nothing to stop them.

While each of the physicians on this particular program had indeed undergone treatment and rehabilitation to overcome his or her addiction, there were never any professional sanctions imposed against them. Even worse, professional sanctions were never imposed against the colleagues or superiors with whom they worked every day, who watched them coming to work drunk or stoned or hung over, and allowed them to go about their business.

Medical organizations and professional publications routinely discuss the problem of impaired physicians. But there seems to be little effort made to stop it. The AMA—a source one would expect to be sympathetic to physicians and their problems—has estimated that 10 to 14 percent of the nation's nearly 600,000 physicians are alcoholics or drug addicts. An estimate of 15 percent appeared in the *Washington Post* on July 16, 1991. New Jersey's Commission of Investigation reported in 1992 that up to 13 percent of that state's doctors may be addicted to drugs or alcohol, with another 3 percent psychotic or mentally ill.

Nationwide, it is likely that there are between 60,000 to 90,000 chemically impaired individuals with licenses to practice medicine. And the problem doesn't start when they become doctors. It begins much earlier, apparently in medical school. A 1987 study by Rush-Presbyterian St. Luke's Medical Center in Chicago of a midwestern medical school found that nearly 20 percent of the students had drug or alcohol problems. In a 1989 study published in the *Journal of the American Medical Association,* more than half the members of a third-year medical school class said that they had personally observed classmates abusing alcohol or drugs.

Yet in more than thirty years as a doctor and seventeen as a lawyer, I don't know of a single patient being told that his or her physician had a drinking or drug problem. Most of the time, at the point at which cases come to our attention, it is impossible to know whether the malpracticing physician was working under the influence of drugs or alcohol. All we see is the result. One celebrated case made headlines more than fifteen years ago, however, and shocked the medical profession. Twin brothers—prominent New York gynecologists Stewart and Cyril Marcus, both of whom had achieved leadership positions in their profession—were addicted to barbiturates, yet continued to practice at a major New York hospital for several years.

Despite evidence of their addiction and increasingly slipshod treatment of patients at the hospital, no one took steps to report their conduct or protect their patients. Finally, after some time, the hospital withdrew their staff privileges. The Marcus brothers were found dead in their apartment a few days later, one from barbiturate withdrawal, the other apparently from a suicidal overdose.

Not much has changed since then. It is still unusual for hospitals to take action against physicians who are addicts. Drug- or alcohol-impaired physicians probably stand a greater risk of having their drivers' licenses revoked than their licenses to practice medicine. If a doctor happens to be driving a car while intoxicated, and is stopped by a police officer, he can be arrested. There's a good chance he'll have his license suspended. If the same doctor injures or kills someone in an automobile accident, he will stand trial and can end up going to jail.

Yet our society allows these same individuals to practice medicine, to take the lives of their patients into their hands with impunity. If an impaired physician injures or kills a patient, it is usually done in the privacy of a hospital room or in the presence of a few of the doctor's colleagues, who will almost never turn in the offender. When the impaired physician slips up, he leaves behind a victim, but unlike the impaired driver, there's no car wreck at the side of the road. No police officers come to the scene to investigate the damage done by the impaired physician. The only witnesses are fellow doctors and the secret usually never leaves the room.

Ironically, anesthesiologists who, by definition, practice in the presence of other physicians in operating rooms, have the highest incidence of drug addiction, likely because they have the easiest access to hospital drug supplies. On July 29, 1991, *Modern Health-care* reported that, according to facilities that specialize in treating addicted physicians, anesthesiologists are three times more likely than other doctors to become addicts, although emergency-room physicians and thoracic surgeons are also higher-than-average abusers. "It's an alarming thought," said the magazine, "but some operating rooms are staffed with anesthesiologists or anesthesia-related technicians or nurses who are addicted to one of the many potent narcotics readily available to them."

Despite this general acknowledgment within the profession, the subject of impaired physicians remains hidden from public view. How can we have confidence that we will receive competent care, when as many as 15 percent of the profession is impaired? How can we have confidence in the profession itself, when it resists such steps as random drug testing of medical personnel?

In an article in the *Washington Post* (July 16, 1991), Georgia physician James Fugedy, himself a recovering addict who now treats and counsels other addicted doctors, said:

> As one who has had problems with addiction and has been in recovery for the past six years, I know what they're going through. When monitoring is incorporated in the treatment plan, the success rate goes up. . . . Unfortunately, there is no hospital I know of that has a good monitoring program. Random screening is important, but to make a difference, it must

include appropriate administrative and clinical follow-up, requiring much time and effort by those who run hospitals. It remains to be seen whether hospitals are willing to commit the time and resources.

The medical community thus far indicates that it is not ready for this. It argues that such tests are not 100 percent reliable, that they are demeaning, that they hurt morale, that they fail to catch every offender. But where is the concern for public safety? Isn't the public entitled to know if their doctors are reliable? Isn't it bad for morale when the wrong medication is administered to a patient by an impaired physician? Or when an anesthesiologist arrives in the operating room stoned?

If Wall Street brokers, Olympic athletes, government employees, and railroad engineers can be subjected to mandatory drug testing, so can physicians. Also, the medical community and government officials must establish a policy for dealing with doctors once impairment becomes known. Clearly, we must provide treatment, but while they are undergoing treatment, the physicians' licenses must be suspended. And the patients who have been trusting these physicians should have access to this information. No one has a greater right to it. However, on the issue of chemical impairment—as with any other issue that involves medical competence—the medical profession seems unable to see beyond the singular goal of protecting its own.

In the Burt case, the medical community's inaction led us to file a lawsuit against the county medical society itself, charging that it clearly knew of Dr. Burt's activities, that it was legally and morally obligated to stop him, and that they were as guilty as he was. We knew that this would be a difficult case to prove: a landmark that would establish an important legal precedent if we prevailed. It would actually be the first case to hold a physician's peers accountable for failing to take action if they knew he was repeatedly committing malpractice. The lower court dismissed this lawsuit on technical grounds, but we continue to pursue it on appeal. If we are successful, this case will acknowledge that the medical profession is not living up to the standards it professes to set for itself.

There are times when medical societies and other professional groups go further than merely protecting their own. They sometimes take actions and positions on issues that are so contrary to the public interest and their own ethical standards that it is inconceivable. In Michigan over the past two years, Dr. Jack Kevorkian, who has become known as the "suicide doctor," has assisted several of his patients to commit suicide. But when the time came for the Michigan State Medical Society to take a position on such practices, it voted to protect its members rather than the public.

In traditional euthanasia cases, a physician or family member takes an active part in ending the life of a terminally ill individual. Dr. Kevorkian added a new twist. He invented a suicide machine, a device that allows the patient to administer his or her own method of suicide, while the doctor simply observes and advises. He apparently believes that this method allows him to avoid legal liability for the deaths.

Dr. Kevorkian's methods are unusual for another reason. The patients he has helped to end their lives were, in some cases, not terminal. They were in pain, they were depressed, one had multiple sclerosis, but the deaths were by no means inevitable.

We strenuously oppose any form of euthanasia under any circumstances. Someone may believe he is dying from a terrible, painful, debilitating disease, and find a few months later that he was misdiagnosed. New medications and new cures are being developed constantly, and we can never tell when even those diseases that seem the most intractable will be overcome. So even in cases that seem terminal, suicide or euthanasia is no answer.

There is no debate about the Kevorkian cases, however. These people were not dying. They were in pain and they were depressed. They needed counseling and they needed support, not a suicide machine. Every physician in America should be outraged by Dr. Kevorkian's actions. Yet when the Michigan legislature proposed legislation to make physician-assisted suicide a crime, the medical society opposed it, reciting what should by now be a familiar theme: no one, including the legislature and the courts, should be able to regulate physician behavior.

■　■　■

Another example of this propensity of medical groups to look after their own has taken place in New Jersey, where the state medical society has pushed legislation to make it more difficult to revoke a physician's license. Customarily, in actions before state licensing boards—as in malpractice lawsuits and virtually all forms of civil litigation—decisions are rendered on the basis of the "preponderance of evidence." The new proposal would prevent any doctor from having his or her license revoked unless there is presented "clear and convincing evidence"—a much higher legal standard that is normally only required in criminal cases, where defendants face imprisonment and where the burden of proof on the prosecution is much higher than on the plaintiffs in a civil lawsuit. In malpractice cases, when the doctor is virtually always going to deny culpability, the clear and convincing evidence standard is nearly impossible to meet.

This debate is particularly disheartening in light of the fact that New Jersey, which licenses more than 20,000 doctors, imposed only ninety-two disciplinary actions of any kind in 1991. Only ten doctors had their licenses revoked. The medical society apparently believes that ten license revocations out of 20,000 physicians is undue harassment. Well, if this legislation passes, the doctors will surely get what they want: No doctors will ever lose their licenses.

On the national front, the American Medical Association made headlines at its 1992 convention when it declared war against murder and pledged to launch a national campaign against violence. "Murders will continue to increase until we start treating it like a public health problem," one attendee was quoted as saying. "If this were due to a virus, the American people and its leaders would be shouting for a cure," said former Surgeon General C. Everett Koop. They're right. No one can argue with their message.

The cause of this great crusade, this mobilization of resources, is that more than 26,000 people were murdered in this country last year. Twenty-six thousand deaths is certainly a cause for concern. But wouldn't the AMA be better served—and better serve the public—if it expressed outrage on behalf of the 100,000 Americans who die each year from medical abuse and neglect? Shouldn't a medical association feel some obligation to police its own ranks before it tries to police the streets? If the AMA views 26,000 murders as an epidemic, what does it call 100,000 victims of medical malpractice? If it cures violence on our nation's streets, but allows incompetent medical care to kill people in hospitals, is it really doing its job?

The fact is that while ethical principles have been part of the medical culture since the inception of the profession, no one has ever enforced them. Whether the negligent practice is committed by a single practitioner seeing a small number of patients, a prolific physician like Dr. Burt, a small rural hospital or a major medical center, the professional community usually ignores any evidence of malpractice that comes to light.

Indeed, the medical profession has ignored this epidemic throughout its history, and at times has done a lot more than just ignore it. The first effort to measure the quality of hospitals in America began in 1913, when a physician by the name of Ernest A. Codman gave a speech to some of his colleagues in which he described patients—for the first time—as consumers and the delivery of health care as a product much like any other commodity. Hospitals, he believed, should be judged on the basis of quality. And yet, there were no standards in existence to allow for such judgments to be made. If an objective method of determining quality could be developed, he said, hospitals and doctors would be able to measure themselves against it and take whatever steps were necessary to improve themselves. At the same time, patients would have some guidance about which hospitals perform best and which are inadequate.

Sometime after Dr. Codman's speech, the American College of Surgeons was created, with one of its initial missions to develop standards of care for hospitals. Those standards were developed, and in 1918, the college began the process of inspecting facilities around the country. Its hope was to determine current levels of quality, to improve and standardize the delivery of health care, and ultimately to provide valuable information to the public.

On October 24, 1919, members of the American College of Surgeons met at a conference at the Waldorf-Astoria Hotel in New York to go over the results of their landmark survey. Of 671 hospitals they had reviewed, only 89 had passed. Among those found to be substandard were some of the nation's best-known institutions.

The surgeons were shocked by the results. Still, one would think, this was a scientific exercise. They had uncovered a significant problem. By making the results public, they could still have fulfilled their mission. They could have protected the public from the inadequate hospitals and begun to work with these institutions on ways to upgrade their practices and their facilities. They did not do that. Instead, they took the results of their research and threw them into the hotel's furnace.

Today, the responsibility for enforcing quality at America's hospitals has shifted to the Joint Commission on Accreditation of Healthcare Organizations, a group created by the American Medical Association, American Hospital Association, and other professional medical organizations that dominate the commission's board and supply most of its $70 million annual budget. While it is a private organization financed by the medical profession, the commission effectively functions as a regulatory agency. It surveys hospitals every three years and "accredits" those it deems to meet appropriate standards. The federal government uses commission accreditation as its standard for whether a hospital is fit to receive Medicaid funds. And most states accept accreditation as evidence that a hospital meets local licensing requirements.

Yet there is some evidence that this commission, which currently accredits approximately 5,300 hospitals, protects the public no better than the original American College of Surgeons. The commission also refuses to make the results of its visits and reviews of hospitals public, so we have no way of knowing a particular institution's strengths or deficiencies. Even worse, though, are the numerous cases of the commission's providing accreditation for hospitals that provide incredibly substandard care. According to the *Wall Street Journal* (October 12, 1988),

Accreditation masks serious failings in possibly hundreds of the 5,100 hospitals in America inspected and approved by the joint commission. . . .

The joint commission allows dangers to health and safety to go uncorrected for weeks, months and even years. Sloppy, irresponsible hospitals have little to fear from the commission: Punishment in recent years has been nearly nonexistent.

When it finds a hospital to be deficient, the commission informs the hospital of its findings confidentially and works with it quietly to improve its standards. Even when successful, the process of reform can take years. During that time, the hospital maintains its accreditation. None of the findings are made public and no information about the hospital's deficiencies is released. The commission does nothing—even in the cases where hospitals make a legitimate effort at reform and improvement—to prevent patients from becoming victims during the transition.

Several years ago, the federal government commissioned state inspectors to conduct a random review of fifty-eight hospitals accredited by the commission during a one-year period. These inspectors found that one in three of the accredited hospitals was seriously deficient.

The commission contends that hospitals will cooperate with it only if all information is kept confidential. It says it is better to have a hospital under its auspices, where it can work to improve it, than have it unaccredited and on its own. But hospitals will cooperate with the commission or a similar body because they have no choice. They need accreditation to qualify for Medicaid funding, a significant source of revenue, and in many cases they need it to be licensed by their states.

If the commission believes that a hospital's deficiencies are reparable, fine. They should work together to correct them. But in the meantime, let the public know what's going on. If deficiencies are minor, patients will understand and probably continue to use the hospital. If the deficiencies are major, however, they should have the right to decide to go elsewhere. When the hospital makes progress, when it corrects the flaws, let the public know about that as well. Then the accreditation process will mean something.

The Burt case shows that the best way—perhaps the only way under present circumstances—of forcing incompetent doctors out into the open is through the courts. The only way of subjecting these practitioners to public scrutiny, and deterring malpractice is through the public attention attendant to lawsuits and trials. The courts have become the sole policing body for the medical profession, and malpractice lawyers have taken on the role of public prosecutors. Major lawsuits, with the major judgments that go with them, may not completely keep negligent physicians from practicing, but they are the one way that currently exists to deter these individuals from practicing their inept brand of medicine.

Unfortunately, even this system is not perfect. In chapter 2, we described the case of Sheila Howard, who discovered a lump on her breast and was sent home by her physician, after his examination confirmed the presence of a lump, without his ordering a mammogram, a biopsy, or any further tests. After we sued, Dr. Hawkins's insurance company settled the case, thus avoiding a trial. Ms. Howard's family accepted the settlement and Dr. Hawkins went back to work.

Two months later, the family of another of his patients contacted us. Almost exactly the same circumstances had occurred. A woman had been to see Dr. Hawkins. He examined her and found a lump on her breast. He noted it in the patient's chart, and once again he took no action. No mammogram. No biopsy. No need to worry, he told the patient. Go home and schedule another examination in about five months. Again, the patient accepted his direction, probably with some relief, and came back in five months to find that the cancer had spread. Another needless death. Another lawsuit followed and another large settlement, prior to trial.

Three months later, another victim. A third woman killed unnecessarily. Dr. Hawkins's partner in his ob/gyn practice, working in the same office, saw a patient, noted a lump on her breast, and sent her home to wait. Her cancer grew. Another lawsuit and another large settlement prior to trial.

Today both of these doctors are still practicing medicine, still seeing and providing medical advice to patients. No disciplinary action has ever been taken against them. While it has been some time since we have had a lawsuit against Dr. Hawkins or his partner, it would not be surprising to learn that others have been filed. And it would not be surprising to see them in court again one day.

Despite the lawsuits, none of these incidents ever became public. That's because when malpractice cases are settled without a trial, as these were, the attorneys for the physicians and the hospitals always require, as part of the settlement agreement, that neither the plaintiffs nor their lawyers publicly discuss the case. The plaintiffs, who usually have years of suffering and extraordinary expenses ahead of them, need the money. They know that if they reject a reasonable settlement offer, the case may take years to come to trial—they may literally not live to see the case judged. So, though most plaintiffs would love to see the doctor publicly tried and his incompetence disclosed, they accept the settlement as the most feasible way of ensuring that their needs are met. They are legally precluded from publicizing the case, or even telling their neighbors about it.

That's why, even in this book, we use pseudonyms. Although the important facts of these cases are accurate, we mask the identities of the individuals involved in order to protect the interests of our clients and fulfill our legal obligations.

There are other physicians providing substandard care. They are known to their colleagues, they are known in the hospitals in which they practice, and in the medical societies of which they are members. They are known to their insurance companies, which often have to settle significant lawsuits against them. The only ones who don't know about them are their patients.

Over the years, our firm has been involved in thousands of cases; at any given time, we are in the midst of nearly 1,000 active ones. Repeatedly, we see the same perpetrators of some of the worst types of malpractice imaginable. Over the years, we have given a lot of thought to why the medical profession adheres to this code of silence. What is it about this profession that causes it to protect its own at the expense of the public?

Likely, it relates to an attitude ingrained in physicians throughout their education, even prior to medical school. They are the brightest students, they get the best grades, they are able to achieve things, to understand things that others can't. When they study and then practice medicine, they become part of an elite group with a grasp of scientific, medical, and technological concepts beyond the reach of most people.

It's easy for individuals in that position to cross the line from pride and self-confidence to arrogance. It's easy for them to believe that they and their peers are the only ones capable of understanding what it means to be a physician—to hold a life in their hands, to possess the knowledge and the ability to cure disease and heal the injured. Who are laypeople to judge their actions?

It's not hard to imagine how physicians begin to rationalize and turn their back on the problem. Good physicians find it easy to see themselves in the shoes of their less-competent colleagues. They give the accused the benefit of the doubt, even if that risks skirting normal standards. But when the medical profession acts this way, standards lose their meaning. Practitioners gain the freedom to determine what is good medicine and what is not. How then can one doctor turn in another for what he or she believes is malpractice?

Every member of the medical profession should consider this carefully. Think about the cases we've described, and ask whether he or she would have taken any action to stop it if possible. In most cases, if the individual is honest, the answer will be no.

If the AMA wanted to show real leadership on public health issues, it would set as its priority educational programs designed to turn around this type of attitude. However, the AMA cannot do it alone. The entire medical community, from college pre-med counselors and medical school professors to hospital administrators and family physicians, must make this a priority. If this change in attitude took place, lives would certainly be saved. Enforcement by state licensing authorities would always be important, but the job of these boards would be immeasurably easier if they could rely on active assistance from the nation's 600,000 doctors.

This is a massive problem that will not be easy to overcome. It may require a generation, but we must make a start. Every medical student must be taught the importance of acting ethically, and every doctor in America must begin to act that way—not only for the benefit of the public but for the benefit of the profession. Like any other business, the medical profession should want its customers—the public—to have confidence in the quality of its product—health care. Patients should be sure that when they go to a hospital they are going to receive quality care, that they are not going to be treated by someone who is not only incompetent but widely known to be incompetent.

Outside authorities can police the medical profession, and they must. It is a matter of public safety. But only by taking steps to police itself can medical practitioners truly earn from the American people the respect and esteem that they claim the right to.

6

COVER-UP

When we began to investigate the Emanuel Revici case, as we studied his records and finally questioned him under oath in depositions and at trial, we began to suspect that this was more than a simple case of malpractice. We knew that, at Revici's urging, Rena Menska had abandoned her regular physician and refused to undergo surgery. We knew what her physical condition was at the time she began seeing Revici, and we knew how her condition progressed because of evidence we obtained from the two hospitals at which she had been examined. We knew a great deal about what had happened, and we learned more from Ms. Menska's relatives and from other doctors who had treated her. And as we probed further, we found that certain things in Revici's records were not consistent with what we knew to be the facts. That's because, at some point after the patient's death, he doctored his records in an attempt to insulate himself from legal liability.

It is customary, in preparing our cases, to subpoena medical records and other documents from the physicians and hospitals involved. The records we received from Revici, however, were extremely suspicious. They were fuzzy photocopies, with some sections darker than others, and some entries apparently written with different pens. We obtained another subpoena ordering him to produce originals of these records so that we could examine them, but Revici claimed that they were no longer in his possession, that he had given them to the state. When we contacted the state, we were told that that they had never received any such records.

One obvious inconsistency in his records related to Ms. Menska's having died as a result of infection from the radiation treatments she had been given at the hospital. The notation was dated prior to the patient's actual death.

Also, Revici contended that one of the reasons his treatment of Ms. Menska was unsuccessful was that his program requires approximately fifty office visits and that she had seen him only twenty times. On thirty other occasions, she had called him and they had spoken by phone, but that, he said, was insufficient to provide optimal results under the Revici method.

Then there was a key point: a notation dated at a point early in Revici's treatment that her liver was enlarged. If her liver had truly been enlarged at that time, if the cancer had already affected her liver almost two years prior to her death, then it would be impossible to prove proximate cause. Cancer of that kind is almost always fatal, and Revici would be able to claim that, at the time Ms. Menska began seeing him, she was already too far gone to help. If she had cancer of the liver, she would have died regardless of the medical care she had received.

Then there was the matter of the photocopied medical school diploma we discussed earlier.

We questioned Revici on all these issues. He told us that he was certain of how many times he had actually seen the patient— as opposed to phone calls—because when he made reference in his records to a phone conversation, he marked it with a *T*, for *telephone.*

Next to two of those *T* marks, however, were notes saying such things as "tumor softer," and "patient well, better." We asked him to tell how he could have formed an opinion about how soft or hard the tumor was during a phone conversation? Did he do a rectal examination over the phone in which he determined that the tumor was getting softer?

He could not answer those questions. In fact, the notes had not been based on telephone calls at all. Clearly, he must have examined the patient on those occasions and told her in person that the tumor was getting softer. But he had gone back later and changed the records to cover his tracks. He had gone back to her charts after her death and wrote in *T*s next to some of the office visits to make it appear as if she hadn't actually been there.

What about the conclusion he had drawn as to the cause of death? How had he heard about the radiation treatments she was having? From Ms. Menska's brother, he said. What made him think that an infection caused by these treatments was the cause of death? we asked. His own experience as a physician.

He stumbled, however, when we asked him how he could have made this notation in his records a full month before the patient died. Was he clairvoyant? Of course not. He was just a little sloppy in altering his files and he got the dates mixed up.

The next issue was Revici's claim that Menska had had an enlarged liver. This took some time to piece together, but eventually we were able to do it. Remember, Rena Menska had been examined just prior to beginning treatment with Revici. Her physician had diagnosed a small tumor in her rectum. Tests at that time found no involvement of the liver. Several months after she began seeing Revici, her nephew had brought her to the emergency room and she had been admitted there. A sonogram and other tests had been performed. That sonogram—an objective test that would leave no doubt about the presence of cancer—had revealed a normal liver. Suddenly, after the patient's death these records turn up, and in them are notes by Revici referring to an enlarged, possibly cancerous liver months prior to the sonogram showing a normal liver. That's impossible. A sonogram and examinations by several physicians proved it. Obviously, the cancer had not spread to the patient's liver until much later. This was another falsehood perpetrated by Revici.

But we had to prove it to a jury in a court of law. During the trial, when we finally had Revici on the witness stand, we examined him vigorously. We pressed him on the question of the enlarged liver.

How was it possible that the liver had been enlarged when he examined this patient and was normal months later when a sonogram was done? He didn't know, he said. He could only describe what he had found.

When he found that the liver was enlarged, we asked, what did he think was the cause of it? Did he believe at the time that it was cancer? He wasn't sure, he answered, there were other things that could cause a liver to be enlarged.

That answer intrigued us. What could cause a person's liver to become enlarged, we asked? Congestion, said Revici.

We asked the witness to tell the jury his opinion of what caused the congestion. His answer: hot sauces. This was certainly a new one for us—someone who claimed to be a doctor sitting on the witness stand and swearing under oath that he believed that an enlarged liver could be caused by hot sauces. So we pursued it.

What did he mean by hot sauces, we asked. Hot in temperature or spice? Spice, he told the jury.

What type of spices specifically did he believe caused an enlarged liver? Pepper, he said.

Was he telling the court, we asked, that in restaurants around the country, as waiters bring pepper mills to diners' tables, they should warn their customers that this is a toxic substance? He waffled on that question, but the point had been made. We had managed to add another page to the Revici scientific analysis of cancer. Pepper caused enlarged livers.

It was a simple matter from that point to show that he didn't understand what causes livers to become enlarged, he wouldn't know an enlarged liver if he saw one, and in any event, he didn't see one in Rena Menska because her liver didn't become enlarged until many months later. If this patient had been treated by conventional means from the start, she might still be alive today. Her liver became enlarged because after time it became cancerous, in the same way her vagina and colon became cancerous.

After Revici killed this poor woman, he compounded his crime by doctoring his records and presenting us with phoney copies, then he compounded it by perjuring himself. On the one hand, a witness like Revici, who destroys himself with his own testimony, is ideal for a trial lawyer. But I must admit that there were moments during our cross-examination when it was difficult to continue with a straight face.

It was at this point that we began to wonder about the issue of his medical training. It was hard to believe that someone who had been to medical school—any medical school—could believe that spices cause enlarged livers. We had several conversations with the New York State Health Commissioner, who was as concerned about Revici as we were. He was also upset that Revici claimed that the Health Department had taken the originals of his records and his diploma, which it had not. The commissioner began his own investigation and, though it was clear that Revici had been licensed to practice medicine by New York in 1947, it was not clear whether he had ever produced an original medical school diploma. Whether he received an M.D. degree from the Institute de Pharmacia y Medicine, or was a pharmacist as we suspected—or whether he fabricated his distinguished past completely—is still a mystery.

What we can say for certain, however, is that Revici's crimes may have been horrendous, but they are by no means unique. We have already described the pervasive attitude in the medical profession that protects incompetent practitioners. But the most egregious cases we see involve not only negligence but deliberate conspiracies and cover-ups. These are in an effort to prevent patients and their families from ever knowing that they were victims of malpractice. Often these cover-ups occur after malpractice lawsuits are filed, with doctors going through old medical records and trying to make it appear as if no malpractice happened.

At a 1977 hearing of the New York State Assembly Committees on Insurance and Health, witnesses testified that forged records are a factor in as many as 10 percent of the lawsuits filed against doctors and hospitals. And that represents only a small percentage of all the forgery that goes on. Only about 10 percent of all incidents of malpractice ever result in lawsuits, and one of the reasons is that physicians and nurses routinely alter records when mishaps occur to make them appear to have been unavoidable.

We've had nurses tell us of obstetricians routinely entering false Apgar ratings—the scale of 1 to 10 that rates the health of a newborn infant—into their records when babies are born injured or brain damaged. One nurse told us that, on one such occasion, when the doctor told her to put down an Apgar rating of 9/10 (9 at one minute after birth and 10 after five minutes), and it was obvious that the infant was severely damaged—perhaps a 1 or 2— she questioned him on it. Don't worry, he told her, it's for legal reasons. That was probably true, although not the way he meant it. Phony records provide a shield that protects doctors from legal action, or from being disciplined or held accountable in any way for their actions.

The New York Assembly Committees heard from a doctor who admitted to changing records. When a patient suffered a head injury in an automobile accident, the physician failed to perform neurological tests and discharged the patient without informing him to watch for any symptoms of blood clots or neurological damage. The patient went home and within a few days was read-mitted in critical condition. He did have a blood clot on the brain. Emergency surgery was performed—surgery that could have saved his life if it had been performed during his first hospital stay. At this point, however, it was too late. He died.

Afterward, the doctor changed his records to indicate that he had done a neurological examination and that there had been no sign of a clot. He also recorded his having given the patient detailed instructions about what to do in the event that various symptoms occurred. It was only because the patient's lawyer had managed to obtain a copy of the original records that the truth came to light.

The deputy director of the hospital where this malpractice and forgery occurred also testified at this hearing that his institution had done nothing to discipline the physician, adding, "I don't think that making a change is unusual." He also commented that he believed that anyone wearing a white coat could probably walk into his hospital's record room and remove a patient's chart.

A nurse told these legislators about a night she came on duty and was told by the nurse she was relieving that the doctor had punctured the patient's lung while trying to get into a vein. This accident happens occasionally, even to the most diligent doctors.

It is not malpractice and the damage is easily corrected if recognized promptly.

The relief nurse told the first to note what had happened on patient's chart. But the nurse who had witnessed the accident hesitated, then called a supervisor. "Write nothing," they were told. "You saw nothing. You heard nothing."

"She wrote nothing," the nurse testified. "There wasn't even a notation on the nurse's notes that the doctor was there that evening. The doctor wrote nothing on his progress notes that would indicate that he had been there. . . . The patient was in distress and a chest tube should have been put in to reinflate that lung. I charted all the signs and symptoms. . . . The following morning . . . he was moved to the intensive care unit, where he died."

The greatest tragedy here is that there was no need to cover up the original error. No one would have blamed the doctor for this slip up. The lung could easily have been reinflated and the patient likely would have recovered. The patient in this case was killed by the cover-up, not the doctor's original mistake.

Regrettably, this type of conspiracy happens with a frequency that would make many criminals envious. Since doctors don't report other doctors, and there is no meaningful process for investigating medical misconduct, the practice of forging records is rarely discussed. If the medical profession won't report or take action against incompetent doctors, surely it is not going to do anything to stop the forging of records. It is a slippery slope from overlooking negligent behavior to believing that negligence is acceptable. Once negligence is deemed acceptable, it is only a small slide further to accepting forgery and perjury.

If some physicians think they are above being disciplined, then why should they be held accountable in court or anywhere else? Self-preservation is a normal instinct in all of us, but covering up acts that cause deaths or injuries is a crime. Committing malpractice is bad enough, but forging records and lying under oath puts these doctors in the same category as muggers and embezzlers.

What's worse it that they usually have partners in crime. Doctors don't function in a vacuum. In a hospital, there are other doctors and nurses around and someone usually knows when malpractice occurs. Likewise, they know when records have been altered to protect someone from liability. But often they turn their backs on this practice, and some actively participate in it.

A Georgia couple, George and Darlene Cochrane, were victims of just such a cover-up. George was an Army E-5 (the equivalent of a corporal) and moved around a lot, so neither he nor Darlene had had a long-term relationship with a physician. In fact, they had just been relocated to an army base in upstate New York when Darlene became pregnant. One of her neighbors, also an army wife, recommended that she see Dr. Bernard Powell. She and George did see him, he seemed all right to them, and Darlene maintained a regular schedule of examinations right through her pregnancy.

Finally, during an office visit, Dr. Powell told Darlene that he thought she was going into labor. He told the couple to go to the hospital immediately, which they did, and he called ahead, arranging for a labor room and instructing that Darlene be put on Pitocin. She remained in the hospital for about eight hours, having induced contractions. Dr. Powell, who had not been to the hospital during this time to examine her, ordered her discharged by phone.

The next day, during a phone conversation, the doctor told Darlene to go back to the hospital. Again he ordered Pitocin to induce contractions. Again she lay in a labor room for eight hours. Dr. Powell never examined her. Finally, he telephoned and had her discharged.

Astonishing as it may seem, the same pattern was repeated for a third day. Darlene was readmitted and given Pitocin, but this time Dr. Powell also ordered X-rays of the pelvis to determine the position of the fetus. However, he never came to the hospital to review them or to see his patient.

At the end of that third day, approximately nine hours after the X-rays were taken, Dr. Powell's partner stopped in to the labor room to see what was going on. He looked at the X-rays. He saw that this was a face presentation—the child's head was not positioned properly for delivery. A cesarean section needed to be performed immediately. He telephoned Dr. Powell, who finally appeared.

Dr. Powell and his partner decided to perform the cesarean together, with the assistance of a pediatrician they called in—a pediatrician to whom they frequently referred patients, someone they felt they could rely upon.

A cesarean section performed with a face presentation is not usually very complicated. This surgery, however, turned out to be more difficult than the doctors expected. They could not remove the baby—it was stuck. Over the past three days, while the patient lay unexamined, the Pitocin had been inducing contractions that were causing the head of this badly positioned fetus to be rammed repeatedly into its mother's pelvis. The two obstetricians pulled and tried to maneuver the fetus, but they couldn't remove it.

Finally, Dr. Powell grabbed one of the baby's arms and his partner grabbed the other, and they pulled. They dislodged the infant, but in the process destroyed the nerves in her arms and irreparably crippled her. How did they explain this nightmare to the parents afterwards? They didn't. They went about their business as if nothing had happened.

The Cochranes, unaware at first that anything was amiss, continued to use for the next three months the pediatrician whom Dr. Powell had brought into the delivery room. Despite regular examinations, this physician never gave the parents any reason to think their child was anything other than normal. At that point, George was transferred back to Georgia, and naturally his family relocated with him.

It was shortly thereafter that they realized their little girl was injured. Although they weren't sure what had happened, they could tell that their daughter couldn't move her arms normally. Their pediatrician in Georgia immediately recognized the severe damage that had been done.

The Cochranes instinctively felt that something had gone wrong during the delivery. The long periods of time in the labor room, the difficulty with the delivery itself—they began to realize that their doctors had not told them the truth.

But when they, and later we, questioned the individuals involved—two obstetricians, a pediatrician, and a total of ten nurses who had been involved in the case from labor through pediatrics—they all lied about it. Each swore under oath that nothing unusual had happened during the delivery, that the baby had been normal at birth. The pediatrician testified at trial that during those three months she had treated the child, she had seen nothing wrong. Then she went a step further, suggesting that the cause of the damage to the child must have been parental abuse that had occurred after the Cochranes moved back to Georgia.

We pored over the medical records. Finally we found something: a note in the nursery records saying "R [right] hand appears flaccid." We knew then that we were onto something. We went back to the parents and went over every aspect of the case with them, forcing them to relive in detail the awful time in that hospital. Almost as an afterthought, Mr. Cochrane mentioned the baby pictures.

Mr. Cochrane was a photography buff. This was their first child. Every day that his wife and daughter had been in the hospital after the delivery, he had been there taking pictures.

So we blew up the photos. They clearly showed the child's arms hanging limp. It should have been obvious to anyone with any medical knowledge that her arms were damaged. One picture showed the mother holding the baby in her room, with the telephone on the stand next to her. We blew this up large enough to see the phone number—the hospital's phone number—so there could be no mistaking the location. The abuse to this little girl had been inflicted not by her parents at home but by two negligent obstetricians during labor and delivery.

When we showed these pictures to the doctors and their legal team, they were mortified. They had believed that if they all stuck with their story, they would never be found out. Confronted with the evidence, they settled the case immediately. The Cochranes received a sufficient amount of money to take care of their crippled daughter. The insurance company paid, and the doctors and nurses who committed malpractice and perjury went scot-free. The child is crippled for life and will never have normal use of her arms or hands.

We saw this type of deceit again in the orthopedic case we described in chapter 2. Dr. Kwan had put a cast on Sean O'Connor's hand too tightly, cutting off the blood supply. He had prescribed codeine for this teenager's pain and sent him home with instructions to hang a hook from his ceiling and elevate his arm from it. The doctor saw the patient's hand become cold and discolored, but did nothing until it was finally lost to gangrene and had to be amputated.

After Dr. Kwan's incompetence cost this patient his arm, what was the good doctor's first act? He changed the medical records to indicate that he had removed the cast much earlier, at the first sign of trouble, and that the ensuing complications were the result of other factors.

Unfortunately for Dr. Kwan, he was about as skillful a forger as he was a doctor. Rather than destroying the original records and writing out an entirely new version, he tried to erase certain sections and write over them. But his extensive erasures wore through the paper, so he typed up new versions of certain sections on separate pieces of paper, cut them out, and pasted them on top of the handwritten originals. But he did it so sloppily that some of his previous handwritten comments were still visible around the edges of the pasted-on typewritten sections. When we held these documents up to the light and read what was underneath Dr. Kwan's sloppy cut-and-paste job, it was simple to find out what had actually happened.

Sometimes we uncover the doctored records early in the investigative process, which usually leads to a settlement. Once it is discovered that the physicians tried to cover something up, the last thing they want is to go to trial. Sometimes, however, we obtain crucial evidence during the trial and the drama unfolds in court through the examination and cross-examination of the perpetrators.

That's what happened when we represented the husband of a twenty-five-year-old woman who had undergone a hysterectomy. She was led to believe that, given her condition, surgery was an absolute necessity. In any event, she was told, hysterectomies are extremely common, surgeons are very familiar with them, and they involve only a small degree of risk. But things did not go quite that smoothly. Inexplicably, almost immediately following the surgery, she went into convulsions. Within three hours her brain stopped functioning. She was put on a respirator in a coma. Two weeks later, she died.

This was a mystery, nearly impossible to unravel. The patient had no family or personal history of seizures. According to the anesthesia report, nothing had occurred during surgery to account for what had happened. This woman had lost only 50 cubic centimeters of blood during the surgery, and her blood pressure never varied. We consulted numerous medical experts and no one could provide a theory.

Since she had been on a respirator for two weeks, her medical records were several inches thick. We sent these files out for review to some of the country's top medical minds. No one could figure it out. We went through the files ourselves, but could find no rational explanation for her convulsions, her brain damage, or her death. This proved to be one of those cases in which our own medical training made the difference.

As the trial approached, we continued to pore over the medical records looking for any evidence that would begin to solve the puzzle. It finally appeared in the form of a small laboratory slip that we had overlooked amidst the dozens of other routine and irrelevant lab slips.

The patient's hemoglobin, or blood count, prior to surgery was 13.5, well within the normal range. The lab slip we uncovered showed that two days after the surgery, while she was still on life support, her blood count was only 6.7. That meant that at some point she had lost more than half the blood in her body. In this case, that would have meant losing about 2,000 cubic centimeters—the equivalent of two quarts of blood.

We went to the autopsy report and found no indication of any blood deposits in the body, as there would have been if the bleeding had taken place following surgery. That left only one possibility. The sole place the blood could have been lost was in the operating room during this "routine" surgery.

The next step was a more thorough review of the anesthesia report. During surgery, blood pressure and pulse rate are monitored constantly and noted on the anesthesia record every five minutes. If a patient loses as much blood as this one had, the blood pressure would drop and the pulse rate would increase. Both would have been noted on the anesthesia record. But that is not what we found. This patient's anesthesia record showed a straight line—as if a perfectly normal operation had occurred, with minimal blood loss. It showed the pulse rate and blood pressure as constant during the entire three-and-a-half hour operation.

We knew then what had happened. The anesthesia report had been falsified. The patient had lost too much blood during surgery. The supply of oxygen carried by the blood to her brain had been severely reduced. This shortage of oxygen is what caused her seizures and the brain damage that killed her. After the surgery, someone changed the records to make it appear as if nothing unusual had happened. What is particularly tragic is that a patient on the operating table need not die from loss of blood, even as great a loss as this one. If the anesthesiologist notices the changes promptly, the surgeon can replenish the blood without damage occurring. For some reason, that didn't happen in this case. In this case, the patient lost a vast amount of blood, yet it went unnoticed and uncorrected.

We got the anesthesiologist on the witness stand and confronted him. Hadn't the patient indeed lost a vast amount of blood during surgery? Hadn't this loss of blood caused her brain damage? Shouldn't this have been recorded in the anesthesia record? Why did his records show a straight line?

The witness broke down and made an incredible admission. He had been in the operating room for the beginning of the surgery, but he didn't see any need to remain for the entire time. He left and went to lunch. He returned for the conclusion of the surgery and really couldn't say what had happened.

The case went to the jury and we obtained a substantial verdict. The insurance company paid an amount that provided our clients with at least some financial compensation for their loss. The anesthesiologist went back to work. As far as we know, he has not missed a day since.

This type of result is consistent from case to case. Even when we prove that a doctor altered a patient's records to cover up a medical error, there is rarely if ever any action taken against him. No matter how damning the evidence, no matter how explosive the testimony during the trial, it is virtually never followed by a criminal investigation. In fact, we sometimes get the feeling that the disciplinary authorities are not even interested.

Ralph Pinto was a fifty-seven-year-old retired public school teacher. A single man, he still lived in the same neighborhood as his two elderly parents and was happy to be able to spend some time taking care of them at this stage in their lives.

For several years, Mr. Pinto had had an arrhythmia, or irregular heartbeat, but he took his medication and was determined not to let it interfere with his life. Like many civil service employees who obtain health insurance coverage through their unions, Mr. Pinto was a member of a health maintenance organization, or HMO, whose office and the hospital with which it was affiliated were conveniently located near his home. He had been in the care of Dr. Sam Demarest, an internist, who had been monitoring the patient's heart trouble for some time. Dr. Demarest was very familiar with Mr. Pinto's overall health history.

After suffering some rectal discomfort on and off for a period of time, Mr. Pinto sought the opinion of his physician and was told that he had a bad case of hemorrhoids. Dr. Demarest recommended that Mr. Pinto check into the hospital for surgery to remove them. This was minor surgery, he told the patient, very simple and very routine. Nothing at all to worry about. And it was the fastest, surest way to get rid of the problem.

That was mistake number one. Surgery is never nothing to worry about. There are many other nonsurgical methods of treating hemorrhoids that should have been attempted first. Certainly, a patient with a history of heart trouble should not undergo surgery unless it is absolutely necessary. But Dr. Demarest cleared him and arranged for him to be admitted for a laser hemorrhoidectomy.

The patient's medical records contain a reference to his arrhythmia, so there is no doubt that the surgeon, anesthesiologist, and other medical staff were aware of it. In fact, there is a note that Dr. Demarest recommended a postoperative electrocardiogram to monitor the patient's heart condition.

The surgeon in this case was Dr. Rahmed Salam. A spinal anesthesia was administered. The surgery—supposed to be quick and simple—took approximately one and a half hours, an outrageous amount of time to keep someone with a heart condition on the operating table. Worse, the vagus nerve, which runs from the brain to the rectum, passes through the chest and affects the heart rate. When the rectum is stretched, as it would have been during a hemorrhoidectomy, the vagus nerve is stimulated and a strain is placed on the heart.

Following surgery, one would expect that a patient with Mr. Pinto's history would not only be given an EKG, as Dr. Demarest had recommended, but would be placed in a cardiac care unit where his heart rate and other vital signs could be monitored constantly. Instead, he was placed in the usual private room, no EKG was ever taken, and nothing more than routine monitoring by the nurses was ever done. He remained in the hospital overnight. The next morning, he was found dead.

We are currently piecing this case together, but here is what we know thus far. During the day of the surgery, Mr. Pinto seemed to be doing well. He had a urinary retention problem—not unusual following this type of surgery—and had to have his bladder emptied via catheter. There are a series of nurses' notes in the patient's chart. At 10:30 A.M., he was doing well. His blood pressure, the notes indicate, was normal, 130 over 90.

There is no other notation in the chart for the rest of the day. Apparently Mr. Pinto was not examined during that time, nor were his vital signs taken. Then there is a note marked 3:00 A.M., saying only that the patient's urinal is empty. The nurse indicated that the urinal was located near the patient's water pitcher and that she told him not to keep it there in the future. There is no mention of his physical condition or any vital signs.

The next notation, at 5:40 A.M., is that the patient had died. Among other things, these notes indicate that at that time, the patient's body was cold and stiff and that rigor mortis had set in. This last notation was indeed true. The family told us that the body was so deformed by rigor mortis that it could not be straightened out by the funeral home. Mr. Pinto had to be buried lying sideways.

It is physically impossible for the patient to have been alive at 3:00 A.M. and to have died and rigor mortis set in by 5:40 A.M. The earlier reference must have been a forgery. Mr. Pinto's physicians and the hospital staff had not only ignored his heart condition and performed possibly unnecessary surgery, but failed to monitor his condition after the surgery and failed even to examine him during the day and night that followed. When he was discovered dead, they went back and filled in some notations in his chart to make it appear as if they had been somewhat more diligent.

Now, Mr. Pinto had never told his parents that he was going to have surgery. He didn't want to worry them unnecessarily. He believed that he would be home in a day, and that they would not have a chance to miss him. But they were used to hearing from their son almost every day, and when they were unable to reach him, they became concerned. It was then that a telegram arrived, informing them that their son was in the hospital and providing instructions if they wanted to visit him. They went to the hospital immediately. When they asked for their son, however, there seemed to be some confusion. At first, the hospital seemed unable to locate him. Then, a nurse told them that Mr. Pinto had been discharged.

That didn't make any sense, since they had just received a telegram saying that he was in the hospital. How could he have already been discharged? They insisted on seeing a doctor. After waiting for quite a while on a busy hospital floor, they were introduced to Dr. Salam, who told them what had happened: Their son had died from cardiac arrest, owing to his arrhythmia. It was unforeseen, he said, and could not have been helped.

The elderly couple was stunned. When they'd seen their son just a day earlier, he was perfectly healthy. Now they had lost him. They went back home to suffer their grief and try to figure out how to go on with the rest of their lives. Ralph had always taken care of them; his pension had helped to support them. What would they do now?

The following day they received a second telegram from the hospital, this one informing them that their son had died. They didn't know what to do, but they wanted to understand what had happened. They could not accept that Ralph had died as a result of hemorrhoids. They decided that they wanted to have an autopsy performed, and contacted the coroner's office, which was holding Ralph's body, to find out what arrangements needed to be made. But the coroner talked them out of it. He had spoken to the surgeon, he told them. He knew the cause of death. What was the point of probing further? Ralph was a good Catholic, as were they. Why not just let him go to his rest? Hadn't he suffered enough? We may never know the coroner's precise motivation—he admitted to the Pintos that he had spoken to the surgeon—but having a conversation like that, talking a family out of having an autopsy performed in such a questionable death, is highly inappropriate. And it simply added another layer to the cover-up of Ralph Pinto's death.

Fortunately the hospital records, to whatever degree they have been doctored, do state that the cause of death was cardiac arrest due to arrhythmia. By admitting knowledge of the patient's prior arrhythmia, they have made our job of proving liability much easier. If they knew of his heart condition, they should have monitored him. Had they monitored him instead of leaving him unexamined for more than eighteen hours, he probably would not have died.

When this case came to our attention, in addition to beginning to prepare a lawsuit, we filed a complaint with the state health department and found ourselves adding a frustrating epilogue to an already disturbing story. The complaint documented our theory that the records had been falsified in an effort to conceal the hospital's culpability. Nothing happened. We called to follow-up. No reply. We telephoned continually, month after month. Finally, we were told what the problem was. A health department official said that there were so many complaints against this hospital that they didn't know what to do. They simply couldn't get to them all in a timely fashion. We would have to wait our turn along with everyone else. That patients were dying unnoticed, that records were being forged, seemed to be of little concern.

Despite codes of ethics in professional medical groups, penalties are almost never imposed against doctors, nurses, and hospitals who either forge records or allow them to be forged. The watchdogs may be sleeping on the job as far as malpractice, negligence, and incompetence go, but forgery of medical records to conceal such behavior makes things even worse. Forgery is more than negligence; it is willful and should be at least as much a criminal offense as forging a check. Doctors who forge medical records are committing fraud, denying the rights of people who have no way of defending themselves or obtaining justice. Every state legislature should enact mandatory criminal penalties for forgery of medical records. If they fail to do so, Congress should act. Physicians who are forgers deserve to have their licenses revoked and— in some cases—be locked up in jail.

If society did impose a stringent deterrence, Linda Simons might still be alive today. We mentioned earlier that we ordinarily don't take on cases that involve cosmetic surgery. But sometimes, as Linda Simons found out, being unhappy with your looks can kill you.

150 / LETHAL MEDICINE

Ms. Simons wanted to have a nose job—or rhinoplasty—and she went to a plastic surgery center she remembered seeing in the newspaper. She met with a pleasant young doctor who explained the procedure to her, discussed how she would like her nose to look after the surgery, and introduced her to his partner, who would assist in the surgery. She excitedly scheduled an appointment for the following week.

The common practice for these operations is to put the patient to sleep with a general anesthesia. Then cotton swabs soaked with cocaine are placed into the patient's nose to constrict the blood vessels and reduce bleeding during the surgery. These swabs are left in the nostrils only for a limited time—long enough for the cocaine to have the desired effect—then removed.

Ms. Simons's surgery began as usual. The physicians inserted the cocaine-soaked swabs into her nose and began to operate. But they forgot to take the swabs out. They went right on with the operation, ignoring the swabs until so much cocaine had been absorbed into her blood that it literally caused an overdose and she died of cardiac arrest.

Of course, the doctors denied everything. The patient had died of cardiac arrest, they said, but it had nothing to do with them. If there was cocaine in her blood, she had ingested it herself, prior to the surgery. Her own drug use had caused her death, they claimed.

This is another case in which the ineptitude of the physicians was consistent throughout. They were not only bad doctors but bad liars as well. When Ms. Simons's body arrived at the morgue, the swabs were still lodged in her nose. The doctors' explanation now became more convoluted. These were not the cocaine-soaked swabs, they said. They had been removed as they should have been. These were saline-soaked swabs they had inserted later. Even when laboratory analysis revealed the presence of cocaine on the swabs, they stuck to their story, contending that the cocaine present in the patient's blood prior to surgery had been absorbed by their saline swabs.

This was an obvious physical impossibility and was easily disproved. For cocaine to have been seeping out of the pores in her nose she would have had to "saturate" her body by taking more cocaine than it is possible for a human being to ingest. And if it were possible to ingest that much cocaine, the patient would have died of an overdose instantly, not have presented herself at the hospital for a nose job.

The matter of altered medical records has been a part of more court cases than can be imagined. Since testimony of this kind obviously is damaging to the physicians and hospitals involved, defense attorneys have sometimes sought to prevent juries from hearing it. They have argued that the issue involves only whether or not malpractice occurred. Whether or not the records were doctored, they contend, is irrelevant. But the courts have ruled that such evidence is relevant. In many cases, the accused doctors themselves open the door to it. The principal reason for their having forged the records was to build a defense. When they refer to the events that transpired, as reflected in their medical records, it is reasonable for the plaintiff's lawyers to attack those records if they are suspected to be a fraud.

In the Kentucky case of *Seaton* v. *Rosenberg*, the patient, Mr. Seaton, sustained brain damage as a result of cerebral anoxia—a shortage of oxygen to the brain—during surgery. This situation is similar to the one described earlier in this chapter that resulted in the death of the hysterectomy patient. Mr. Seaton and his family sued his anesthesiologist, Dr. Rosenberg, for malpractice.

Once the suit was filed, the Seatons' attorney notified Dr. Rosenberg and the hospital at which the surgery took place that he would like to examine the patient's hospital records. Dr. Rosenberg immediately went to the hospital record room, requested Mr. Seaton's file, and began making changes. He "reviewed" the patient's anesthesia record, making whatever additions he felt appropriate, until the clerk in charge of the record room realized what the doctor was doing, told him that making such alterations was improper, and asked him to stop.

Dr. Rosenberg's defense argued against admitting evidence of the doctor's forgery, but the Kentucky Supreme Court said that such after-the-fact alteration of medical records was unusual behavior that should be considered at the trial. The jury, the court ruled, could attach whatever significance it deemed appropriate to the doctor's behavior.

The Seaton case was one in which it was clear that the doctor had altered the patient's records: There was a witness, the records clerk. In most cases, it's not that easy to figure out.

Michael Berger was a judge who lived with his wife, Celia, a nurse, in Staten Island, New York City. Celia Berger had been experiencing weakness in her legs for some time. One evening lying in bed, she realized that her legs were numb. Her husband helped her to the car and took her to the hospital. After an examination in the emergency room, Dr. Michael Vincent, a neurosurgeon, diagnosed Ms. Berger as having bleeding that was causing pressure on her spinal cord.

Immediate surgery is indicated in such cases. The longer the pressure on the spinal cord continues, the greater the risk of permanent neurological damage. Dr. Vincent decided to transfer the patient to another hospital—one more than an hour away in Manhattan. After seeing her into the ambulance and on her way, he left the hospital and went home to bed.

Ms. Berger was admitted to the second hospital, but was left waiting in the emergency room all night, with no treatment administered until the following morning. At that time, the hospital's chief of neurosurgery was notified about her condition, and recognizing the risk of delay, operated immediately. The overnight delay, however, had taken a toll. The spinal cord was permanently damaged, and Ms. Berger's ability to use her legs is now significantly impaired.

When Judge and Ms. Berger came to us, we knew right away that this was a clear case of malpractice. A delay of more than twelve hours when a patient presents herself with compression of the spinal cord is gross negligence. But where precisely did the negligence lie? Dr. Vincent had diagnosed her correctly, and claimed to have taken what he thought was the prudent action of sending her to a hospital that was better equipped to handle the surgery. The chief of neurosurgery at the second hospital had operated as soon as he realized the patient's condition. The negligence was in the delay, and we needed to find out why that delay had occurred.

We uncovered only one piece of relevant evidence that related to this question prior to the trial, and at first we were not quite sure of its meaning. There was a surgical consent form, signed by Ms. Berger, that had been obtained by Dr. Vincent at the Manhattan hospital. What was he doing at this hospital obtaining a consent form when he claimed that his care of this patient ended the previous night?

This question remained unresolved until trial, when we were able to examine Dr. Vincent on the witness stand. At first he stuck to his story, but under tough questioning he finally responded truthfully. After transferring Ms. Berger to the second hospital, he had intended to join her and perform the surgery himself. He went home to get a good night's sleep, thinking that the surgery could wait until morning. The second hospital did not make any attempt to perform surgery earlier because the staff was expecting the patient's doctor to arrive and perform it.

When Dr. Vincent finally arrived at the hospital, he had Ms. Berger sign the consent form and asked the hospital staff to reserve an operating room for the surgery. At this point, however, he was informed that he would not be allowed to perform this surgery because he did not have privileges in that hospital. Customarily a physician must be recognized by a particular hospital—he must have "privileges"—in order to treat patients there. Dr. Vincent did not have privileges. He had requested them of this hospital recently, but they had not yet been approved. Apparently the young man believed that he could simply walk into the hospital and be allowed to perform surgery. He was turned away. It was at that point that the hospital's chief of neurosurgery became involved and decided to perform the surgery himself.

Nowhere were any of these events recorded in the files. There was no record that Dr. Vincent ever appeared at the second hospital. There was no record of his having been turned away. There was no explanation of why the patient remained in the emergency room for an entire night. And when asked about it under oath, Dr. Vincent's first response was to lie about it.

We pressed ahead with the trial, and at its conclusion, the jury decided in our favor. But prior to deciding on the size of the award—which is done only after the verdict is rendered—the doctor, the hospital, and their insurance companies offered a settlement of $2 million. The Bergers agreed.

Cover-ups of this nature can have a devastating impact. Once a doctor's malpractice has destroyed a patient, his forgery of records and perjured testimony can destroy a legal case. Since these cover-ups almost always involve conspiracies, they are sometimes nearly impossible to crack.

Eve Constantinos, a healthy thirty-two-year-old woman, went into the hospital to deliver her baby, which turned out to be a perfectly healthy girl. During the delivery, however, Ms. Constantinos suffered a fourth-degree tear from her vagina to her rectum. A fourth-degree tear is quite extreme—the tissue separating the vagina and the rectum is completely torn through. These tears occur from time to time during childbirth; while they are not normal or common, neither are they extraordinary. The principal risk from such a tear is the onset of infection. Usually in these cases, the mother is kept in the hospital for several days until she heals, to be sure that no infection develops. A portion of the wound is kept open during that time, so that it can be drained if necessary.

But Ms. Constantinos's obstetrician just stitched her up tight right after surgery, and sent her home after the usual three-day stay in the maternity ward. She was discharged from the hospital on a Thursday. At that time, she complained to the doctor that she had pain in the area of her buttocks, but he told her not to worry about it. She continued to experience pain during the weekend, but as the doctor had not seemed concerned, she tried to ignore it. By Monday the pain had become more severe, and she returned to the hospital and was readmitted. By Wednesday, the area was not only infected but gangrenous. Surgery was performed. In order to keep the infection from spreading, it was necessary to remove approximately two-thirds of the patient's vagina.

When we obtained the medical records after being retained by Ms. Constantinos and her family, we realized that they were not consistent with what the patient recalled having happened. According to the records of her obstetrician, Dr. William Hevesi, he had told her when he discharged her on Thursday that she was to return for a follow-up examination in two days. She did not come in at that time. When she was admitted to the hospital on Monday, according to these records, there was no problem, no sign of serious infection. On Tuesday, the same—no problem. Suddenly, on Wednesday they discovered the presence of gangrene. A surgeon was contacted immediately, and Ms. Constantinos was in the operating room within two hours. According to Dr. Hevesi and his records, there was nothing more they could have done. First, the patient had not followed instructions to return for her follow-up. When she did come in, she was monitored closely and, at the first sign of trouble, prompt action was taken. The result, they said, was regrettable but unavoidable.

That was the story reflected in the records, and that is the story that Dr. Hevesi and his colleagues at the hospital presented right through the first stages of the trial. On several occasions the judge had asked both sides to discuss the possibility of settling the case prior to trial—a routine judicial effort to avoid the time and expense of a trial—but the defense had consistently refused. They were adamant in their denial of any wrongdoing, and they would not give our clients a penny, they said. Then we came up with some interesting information.

Dr. Hevesi claimed that when he had discharged Ms. Constantinos from the hospital on Thursday, he had told her to return to his office in two days. That would have been a Saturday. We checked discreetly, and found that this doctor's office was not open on Saturdays. As far as we could tell, it had never been open on a Saturday. He had slipped up. We then began to suspect that the medical records we had received—that Dr. Hevesi was basing his defense on—were phonies. And we knew that, in changing these records, he had made at least one mistake: His office was closed on the date he claimed to have told the patient to come in. Perhaps he had made other errors as well.

We went through all our files in minute detail looking for some inconsistency, something that would give us a break. We found it. It was a minor notation, easily overlooked before. The surgeon who had finally operated on Ms. Constantinos had called the hospital on Tuesday—the day before the surgery—to ask the nurse on duty about the patient's condition.

Dr. Hevesi's story was that the patient was fine on Tuesday, that gangrene was discovered on Wednesday, and emergency surgery was scheduled at that time. According to the medical records, the surgeon was not brought into this case—did not even know this patient existed—until Wednesday. If that were true, why would the surgeon call on Tuesday to check on Ms. Constantinos? They must already have been aware of her condition prior to the time that phone call took place. Dr. Hevesi had obviously discussed the case with this surgeon on Tuesday, but rather than schedule surgery immediately, he waited a full day or more—a critical delay in a case like this.

We then learned that Dr. Hevesi's wife had a job with his malpractice insurance company. On a hunch, we subpoenaed their records on this case. Again, we looked for inconsistencies, no matter how small—any documents we might have overlooked that would give us another piece of the puzzle. What we received from the insurance company were files that contained not just a missing clue as we'd hoped, but an entirely different set of medical records. Dr. Hevesi and his wife had taken the original records for the Constantinos case out of the hospital and had buried them in what they thought was a safe hiding place—amid volumes of files maintained by the insurance company. He had then prepared an entirely new set of records, describing the case as he would have liked it to have occurred. And he and his lawyers had voiced moral indignation at any discussion of settling the case.

The original records revealed the true story. Ms. Constantinos had suffered a fourth-degree tear during the delivery of her child.

The doctor had sewed it up and treated her as any other maternity patient. He never considered the possibility of infection and took no precautions to prevent one. He sent her home from the hospital with no particular instructions whatsoever. There was no discussion of any follow-up visit.

When the patient returned to the hospital on Monday complaining of pain, an examination revealed the presence of a severe infection. When an infection like this is involved, time is of the essence. Infections quickly spread and, if untreated, can destroy the area of the body affected. So it was in this case. Nothing was done, no treatment was administered. The infection took a predictable course. Gangrene developed, then finally someone noticed that something was wrong and surgery was performed.

This break in the case came about within a very short space of time and, in fact, we did not have it all prepared by the time the trial started. The day before the trial was a Thursday. On that day, the defense was still as adamant as ever against settling the case. On Friday, we had begun to put this damaging material together, but the trial started. We worked over the weekend and scheduled a conference on Monday with the judge to present to him and Dr. Hevesi the evidence we had obtained of his forgery of records. As soon as we presented proof that the doctor had committed malpractice and that he and his wife had conspired to conceal evidence and alter records, they asked us to consider settling the case. In fact, they practically begged us to settle. They knew that, having come to this point, it would have been no great burden for us to go to trial. They also knew that a trial would generate headlines, that Dr. Hevesi and his wife would be exposed, and that their careers would be destroyed. They would have deserved it. But our first responsibility is to our clients. Trials are always uncertain; you can never be sure of the result. The settlement offer was very generous, and Ms. Constantinos accepted it.

Ms. Constantinos still suffers from constant pain in her abdomen, rectum, and groin area. She has frequent kidney infections, an almost constant discharge, and her bowel and urinary functions are totally unpredictable and uncontrollable. She has a lack of feeling in the area and says that there are times when she bends down and realizes that she has urinated down her leg without knowing it. She has been divorced and, as she cannot work, her only source of income is disability and sporadic child support from her ex-husband. She has virtually no social life and lives in her father's home with her daughter. The lawsuit was settled, but the truth about this physician's behavior never came to light. No disciplinary action was ever taken against him.

This case and others described in this chapter illustrate several important points. First, some medical practitioners apparently feel that they should have immunity from any punishment for their malpractice. Not only do they feel that their actions should not subject them to punishment, but they will go to almost any length to prevent being exposed. In all of these cases, physicians not only were responsible for the death or injury of their patients but they and their colleagues engaged in behavior after the fact that most people would consider criminal. While some cases of malpractice may happen accidentally, the forgery of records and perjury by witnesses under oath are malicious acts purposely designed to protect the physician at the expense of the patient.

It should also be apparent that, contrary to myths the AMA and others try to spread about malpractice attorneys, trial lawyers in this field investigate the facts, question the doctors and other witnesses, and uncover fraud. True, the system is not perfect. Most people who are victims of malpractice don't sue. Most victims of malpractice are also victims of scandalous misrepresentations by members of the medical profession, who routinely lie and mislead patients and their families. Most victims of malpractice are given phony explanations, attributing the problem to unnamed complications, or "God's will," or a host of mysterious and inexplicable phenomena. With rare exceptions, they are never told the truth. They never know if their medical records have been altered. Without attorneys digging into the circumstances of their treatment, they never know exactly what happened.

Even in those cases where a lawsuit is filed, most of the time the case is settled and the perpetrator suffers no penalty or discipline. But at least one victim got to the truth. At least one victim received compensation for his or her pain. And when cases do go to trial, there is at least some opportunity for the general public to see what happened, to learn about the malpractice, and to protect themselves against it in the future.

7

HARD TO KILL MYTHS

The medical profession has a long road ahead if it is to deal with the problems that plague it. Incompetent doctors are destroying patients, many of these individuals forge records to conceal their crimes, and government officials and the profession itself fail to inform or protect the public. If viewed in that light, malpractice litigation could prove to be an aid to the medical profession, exposing substandard practices and practitioners, helping the profession ensure the maintenance of the highest possible standards. In effect, by exposing negligent doctors and pointing out areas in which obvious errors are repeatedly made, lawsuits could be a valuable tool, not only for enforcement but also for the prevention of bad medicine.

Instead, the medical profession seems to view an attack on any doctor, no matter what the offense, as an attack against all. Rather than examine the substance of the issue, its response is usually to attack back. Blame the patients who've been harmed, blame the lawyers who represent them, blame the entire legal system. Blame everyone except the doctors who commit the malpractice. And this pattern of denial and casting of blame is nothing new. Go back more than a century—even before Abraham Lincoln's litigation helped define American law on malpractice. The response has always been the same.

160

In 1847, a physician wrote in the *Boston Medical and Surgical Journal* that "Legal prosecutions for mal-practice occur so often that even a respectable surgeon may well fear the results of his surgical practice."

In 1851, *Medical Examiner* stated: "Mischievous prosecutions for some years have alarmed medical gentlemen in various parts of the country to such a degree that many have concluded to let all surgical patients go unassisted in their afflictions."

A New York physician claimed in the 1850s that "suits for mal-practice were so frequent in the Northern states [that many doctors] abandoned the practice of surgery, leaving it to those who, with less skill and experience, had less reputation and property to lose."

A Pennsylvania doctor of the same period warned "some of the most competent young men are driven off, and such as remain refuse to take responsibility for surgical cases." And a medical publication based in western New York State warned in 1844 that doctors were "constantly liable to vexatious suits, instituted by ignorant, unprincipled persons, sometimes urged on, it is presumed, by those who have a private grudge. . . ."

The warnings were dire: Unless these outrageous lawsuits were stopped, doctors would refuse to treat patients in many specialties. Ultimately, they would stop practicing medicine altogether.

In this context, the myths about malpractice and the degree to which they have become part of the public's consciousness is no mystery: Physicians have been spreading them for more than a century. Millions of dollars are spent each year by organizations representing doctors and their insurance companies in political campaign contributions, lobbying efforts, and advertising and promotional attempts to distract the public from the true nature of this crisis.

Many statements by the medical profession made in the 1840s and 1850s are the same as those being made in the 1990s. For almost 150 years, doctors have been arguing that the threat of malpractice lawsuits is forcing competent physicians to give up their practices, leaving many communities around this country without vitally needed medical services.

In 1850, the argument was that there would be no surgeons left as a result of lawsuits. In the 1990s, we're supposedly driving all the obstetricians out of business. Any time there is a problem with a delivery, they say, any time an imperfect child is born, the doctor gets sued, whether or not it's his fault. Many obstetricians, the argument goes, are sick of worrying about all these unjustified lawsuits, and they're tired of paying ever-increasing malpractice insurance premiums. So they stop delivering babies altogether. Many communities, particularly rural ones, the argument goes, are desperately underserved. Thus, lawsuits are "mischievous." Physicians are going to "abandon the practice" of medicine. Well, it didn't happen then, and it's not happening now.

If obstetricians are abandoning their practices and leaving some communities unserved, it has nothing to do with lawsuits. Doctors go where the patients are. And they work in the specialties—and geographic regions—that are most rewarding. The AMA has noted that physicians in rural areas earn on average about one-fifth as much as physicians in metropolitan areas. So it's not surprising that few young obstetricians wish to locate their practices in rural communities.

Conversely, in Nassau County, an affluent suburb of New York City where obstetricians pay among the highest malpractice insurance rates in the country, there are more obstetricians per capita than almost anywhere else in the country. No shortage of obstetricians there, despite the high cost of insurance. Nassau County has nice communities in which to live and work. The cost of malpractice insurance and the threat of lawsuits doesn't seem to matter nearly as much as the ability to live and work in a good neighborhood.

While indeed there may be a paucity of obstetricians in some rural areas, it is less a result of lawsuits and more a reflection of a natural tendency on the part of physicians—as with anyone else—to locate in the regions with the best quality of life and the most affluent patients.

As far as the cost of insurance goes—even after the cost of malpractice insurance and all other business expenses, office rent, and staff salaries—the average ob/gyn in America earns $207,000, according to the AMA. That compares quite favorably with the average pretax net for all physicians, which, after expenses, is $164,000. Obviously, insurance premiums are not having an undue effect on the ability of obstetricians to make a living.

The truth is that some doctors move away from obstetrics because it is a difficult specialty to practice well. Many doctors get tired of being called to the hospital at all hours of the night and so, as they get older, they stop delivering babies. Undoubtedly, some young medical students are making the decision not to specialize in obstetrics for the same reason.

The medical community points to what it considers a high turnover rate among obstetricians—11 percent per year—and concludes that these doctors must be abandoning their practices because of the threat of malpractice lawsuits. But during the past fifty years, even prior to the recent "malpractice crisis," obstetricians stopped practicing in their specialty at an average rate of approximately 10 percent per year. And most of this turnover relates to the nature of the specialty. When young doctors begin their ob/gyn practices, most of their patients are young women, many of whom are having babies. So a large portion of their practice is delivering babies. As the doctors age, so do their patients. Suddenly, the patients the doctor has been seeing since they were both thirty years old have become middle-aged. At this point, a number of his patients require hysterectomies and other types of surgery, and that becomes a major part of the practice. The physician, who can now maintain a successful practice without the sacrifices one makes in obstetrics, decides to associate with a younger doctor. As younger, pregnant women come in, the older doctor refers them to the associate. The older doctor tells the insurance company that he or she no longer is practicing obstetrics, and they chalk up another statistic. The myth of the vanishing obstetrician is accepted as fact, even at the highest levels of government, as high-powered lobbying groups like the AMA and the American Tort Reform Association spend millions of dollars a year persuading the American public and the media of their veracity.

One of the greatest hoaxes ever put over on the people of this country—and this includes a lot of people in Congress as well as the White House—is the "defensive medicine" myth. Doctors, according to the AMA, conduct costly, unnecessary tests on their patients in order to protect themselves from lawsuits, thus driving up the overall cost of health care. The AMA has said that physicians are performing $15 billion worth of these unnecessary tests on patients each year. They call this defensive medicine. Former president Bush went so far as to claim, in a 1991 speech at Johns Hopkins University, that the cost of defensive medicine was as much as $75 billion.

The cost of defensive medicine is irrelevant because, as the AMA describes it, defensive medicine does not exist. It is a contradiction in terms. If tests are being performed that assist the doctor in determining a diagnosis or treatment, then they are not unnecessary. They are part of a good examination, the patient benefits from them, and they have nothing to do with protection against lawsuits.

If doctors perform unnecessary tests, they are likely doing it for the money. Cases abound of physicians ordering patients to undergo tests and procedures that they don't need, then billing the patient or the insurance company for the additional cost. This practice is nothing new. It used to be called fraud; now the AMA calls it defensive medicine.

Indeed, the financial incentives for engaging in such behavior are great. According to *Medical Economics* (July 1992), internists charged a median fee in 1990 of $110 for a comprehensive office visit, including as much as 45 minutes of the doctor's time, including taking a history, performing an examination, and talking with the patient. For spending ten minutes examining a bowel with a sigmoidoscope, the same internist can earn about $126.

On April 12, 1990, the *Wall Street Journal* reported on a chain of walk-in clinics in Massachusetts where, as part of a study on this subject, doctors were offered financial incentives based on the revenues they generated. In other words, the more patients they saw and the more tests they ordered, the more they got paid. The results: Doctors ordered 23 percent more lab tests per patient visit and 16 percent more X-rays. And they saw 12 percent more patients than they had during the previous year. "The finding," said the *Wall Street Journal,* "isn't surprising, but it adds a new dimension to the controversy over the role of money in medicine. While many businesses use bonuses to increase sales, some health-care experts worry that such incentives can cloud a doctor's judgment in prescribing care for patients."

In fact, such incentives exist throughout the medical profession, as they do in every industry. Hospitals are usually reimbursed by Medicaid and private insurance companies according to something called the DRG system, which, rather than paying according to the length of time the patient is in the hospital, pays a set amount for a specific type of illness. Government investigations have frequently found illnesses redefined in hospital records, as a description is sought of a similar ailment that is eligible for a higher rate of reimbursement. Also, reimbursements are based on the diagnosis of whatever is determined to be the "primary" illness, giving doctors and hospital administrators the ability, in cases where a patient suffers from multiple ailments, to choose the one with the highest reimbursement rate.

According to *Consumer Reports* (July 1992), "since the mid-1980s, doctors have also manipulated the reimbursement system by 'unbundling' services—that is, charging for two or more separate procedures instead of one. For instance, instead of billing $1,200 for a hysterectomy, a doctor can collect $7,000 by billing separately for various components of the operation. Commercial services conduct seminars to teach doctors how to maximize reimbursement in this way. . . ."

For doctors, whose decisions obviously have a great effect on the cost of a patient's hospital care, the more tests, the more they get paid. And there is much discretion left to the physician in subtle judgments and descriptions of procedures that can affect the cost of care dramatically. Following surgery on the foot, for example, should a procedure be described as clipping a toenail and cleaning the surrounding area, or as débridement of the wound?

Débridement is a surgical procedure for which doctor and hospital would receive a significantly higher payment. Which description do you think they choose?

All the unnecessary surgery we described earlier, tens of thousands of cases each year, drives up the cost of health care. Manipulating records and reimbursement formulas drive up the cost of health care. All the misprescribed drugs drive up the cost of health care. Taking care of hundreds of thousands of people injured each year by their doctors also adds a significant amount to the nation's health-care bill. But to blame it on something called defensive medicine is ridiculous.

If such a practice were actually going on, it would not only be bad medicine, it would be a crime. Taking a person's money and using it for one's own purposes—whether it is used to purchase unnecessary tests or to buy a yacht—is embezzlement and fraud. If there truly are doctors who are charging fees for tests that have no value to the patient, then they are taking money for their own benefit rather than for the service they are supposed to be providing. That is a crime and they should be prosecuted for it.

Ironically, there is no way that tests of this nature could have anything to do with lawsuits. If a test is unnecessary, if it is irrelevant to a patient's illness, how could it possibly assist in the defense of a malpractice lawsuit? A lawsuit seeks to show that substandard care led to the injury of a patient. What help is it to a physician in that position to be able to produce irrelevant test results? If the AMA were serious about health-care reform it could perform a valuable public service by producing the names of doctors who claim they are practicing defensive medicine.

There are those who have a slightly different view of defensive medicine, however, taking exception with the AMA's view of this situation. Some people argue that what doctors claim is defensive medicine actually constitutes good medicine. A report in the *Journal of the American Medical Association* (May 22/29, 1987) indicates that, at least in dollar terms, 39 percent of defensive medicine reflects extra time spent by doctors with their patients; 41 percent involves additional follow-up visits after a procedure is performed or a course of treatment is begun; and another 20 percent is spent on additional record keeping.

Given what we have seen as the principal causes of medical malpractice—failing to be present when needed, failing to take a complete medical history, failing to perform a thorough physical examination—it could be that malpractice lawsuits are forcing some doctors to provide better care. They may not like spending more time with their patients or keeping accurate records, but that's what good medicine is all about.

As Dr. Paul Weiler, one of the authors of the Harvard study, was quoted as saying in the May 25, 1992, *American Medical News:* "If we were to find that the tort system [the type of civil lawsuits we are describing are known as torts] was producing more defensive driving, and we asked the public if they supported such an incentive, my guess is that the vast majority, including most doctors, would say it was a good thing." In other words, if defensive medicine means practicing in a way that reduces unnecessary injury to patients, it is beneficial and should be applauded by the medical profession.

When "defensive medicine" is defined by the AMA, it is a difficult concept to accept. In an industry known for producing scientific data, no one has ever produced a study to support the claim that this situation exists, let alone costs the taxpayers $15 billion a year. No one has produced the name of a single doctor who has engaged in this behavior or a single patient upon whom it has been practiced.

Nevertheless, rather than be hindered by a lack of evidence, proponents of this myth rail against the cost of defensive medicine. They try to make the case that malpractice lawsuits add to the country's overall health-care bill because the threat of these suits causes doctors' insurance premiums to rise. We've already debunked this myth as it relates specifically to obstetricians, but this theory is equally indefensible for the medical profession as a whole.

The truth is that of the $823 billion a year that is spent in this country on health care, only $5.6 billion is spent by doctors and hospitals on malpractice insurance. That's less than 1 percent—

not an extraordinary amount. Even at this level, insurance companies are making huge profits on the fees they collect.

The total amount of all malpractice awards in America is less than the interest insurance companies earn on invested premiums. Thus, the billions of dollars paid by doctors in insurance premiums over the years are still in insurance company coffers, leading the General Accounting Office in 1987 to report that liability insurance companies had realized profits in excess of $110 billion during the preceding decade.

And the years since then have been good to these insurers as well. One of the largest companies in the country, St. Paul Fire & Marine Insurance Company, reported a 31 percent decline in malpractice claims from 1985 to 1989. In New York State, the Office of Court Administration reported that, after a steady rise in lawsuits during the preceding decade, there has been a 76 percent dropoff from 1986 to 1991. And while insurance companies have now begun to acknowledge this phenomenon, which is saving them a fortune, by lowering insurance rates slightly, the average cost of insurance has risen by 2 percent during this time. Thus, the profits have continued to pile up. One New York company, Medical Liability Mutual, which started with no assets in 1975, accumulated over $3 billion in assets by the end of 1991, an amount far exceeding any liabilities it might incur.

As we've said, the annual cost of insurance overall—$5.6 billion—is not sufficient to have much impact on America's spiraling health-care costs. Nevertheless, if this is an area that policymakers want to focus on, they should examine the profits made by insurance companies.

The Harvard study commissioned in 1991 by the New York State Department of Health found that the total amount of compensable damages from malpractice—even if all the victims in New York State sued—would be $894 million: $285 million in lost wages and fringe benefits, $103 million in uninsured medical costs, and $506 million in lost household production. By contrast, the malpractice premiums paid by New York doctors and hospitals to insurance companies, plus the amount spent by self-insured health-care providers, amount to more than $1 billion. Thus, even if all these people were compensated fairly for their injuries, the insurance companies would still end up ahead by more than $100 million a year. Since only about 10 percent of malpractice victims actually sue, that leaves these companies way ahead financially.

One might think that huge profits would cause insurance companies to keep a low profile in the national health-care debate. Quite the contrary. Instead, they have taken the offensive and aggressively advanced proposals to limit lawsuits and prevent malpractice victims from receiving significant awards. Not content with the amount of money they already are making, they push for more. Rather than cut the amount of money the unfortunate families of injured parties can receive, we ought to look at reducing that $110 billion in insurance company profits.

It is not only insurance companies that bear the blame for the perception that insurance premiums drive up the cost of medicine. Doctors are guilty as well. About six years ago, the average cost of insurance for an internist in Manhattan rose from $5,000 to $7,500 a year—a fairly steep increase. During that same period, internists raised their fees by an average of $20 per patient visit. Now, a successful internist might have as many as 100 patient visits per week. That amounts to an increase in revenues of $2,000 per week. Over fifty weeks (allowing for a modest two-week vacation each year), that's $100,000. Apparently using the same logic oil companies used to gouge consumers with exorbitant price increases during the Persian Gulf War, these physicians raised their prices by as much as $100,000 a year to compensate for an insurance premium increase of $2,500. And they blame it on lawsuits. Clearly, there is no correlation among the cost of malpractice lawsuits, the cost of insurance, and the cost of health care in America today.

According to the Coalition for Consumer Rights, a consumer advocacy group based in Chicago, all of the costs associated with medical malpractice account for only 1 percent of total health-care expenditures in America. It calls medical malpractice costs negligible as opposed to such factors as inflation, demographics, and the advent of new costly treatments—in addition to limited competition, fraud, and waste among the medical profession. In a 1991 report, the coalition stated, "To the extent that tort law forces doctors to exercise a reasonable standard of care, costly injuries and adverse events are actually limited. . . . Reducing the actual amount of doctor negligence should be the cost-containment strategy for policy makers concerned about medical malpractice."

In other words, if the medical profession is truly interested in reducing the cost of health care in America, it should try to reduce the amount of malpractice that is committed by its members.

When all else fails, "kill all the lawyers," as Shakespeare said. That seems to be the position of the medical and insurance lobbyists. The problem is that they would bury our crippled clients and their families with us. The myth-makers contend that, since most malpractice lawyers have a contingency-fee arrangement with their clients, and the clients have nothing to lose by suing a doctor, the system has become a lottery, with unhappy patients, encouraged by greedy lawyers, taking a chance that they will be able to win a large award.

There may be some incompetent attorneys practicing law, just as there are incompetent physicians. But under normal circumstances, it makes no sense for a lawyer to encourage a client to sue unless he or she truly believes the case to be valid.

As we've explained in chapter 3, bringing a malpractice lawsuit to trial may take years of work, with legal research, investigation of medical information, and depositions by witnesses. We've described the effort that often goes into this process. Apart from the moral and ethical reasons for not bringing a frivolous lawsuit, if we devote all that time and energy to a case and the judge throws us out of court, we don't get paid. Ethics, logic, and economics argue against lawyers bringing unwarranted lawsuits.

Furthermore, when it raises the specter of unfair litigation, the medical profession ignores research that has shown, in fact, that most incidents of clear medical malpractice never result in lawsuits. The Harvard study in New York State demonstrated that in one year there were 36,000 deaths and injuries caused by negligent medical care in hospitals. Of those 36,000, only about 3,000 ever resulted in lawsuits—fewer than 10 percent.

Another survey of malpractice victims in New York State (published in the *New England Journal of Medicine,* July 25, 1991) found that less than 2 percent ever file lawsuits. Russell Localio, a researcher at Pennsylvania State University and co-author of this study, stated: "Our results would suggest that the system of medical malpractice claims does not hold health-care providers responsible for injuries due to substandard care."

Our firm recently won one of the largest individual jury verdicts ever in a medical malpractice case. But even this large award— $21.7 million—will not truly compensate our client. Faced with the prospect of lengthy appeals by the defense—a process that would have prevented her from receiving any payment for several years—our client ultimately settled the case for $4.5 million, still a significant amount of money. But her child was born brain-damaged as a result of medical neglect and incompetence. He is now severely mentally retarded, and will require extraordinary care for the rest of his life.

In many respects, this case was quite typical. The mother went into labor, but her obstetrician didn't show up at the hospital. The umbilical cord became tangled around the fetus's neck and cut off its oxygen supply. The problem was noted on the fetal distress monitor, but the inexperienced resident attending the mother did the wrong thing. Rather than performing an immediate cesarean section, he prescribed Pitocin, stimulating contractions, causing the pelvis to clamp down on the cord and cut off even more the flow of blood and oxygen to the fetus.

The obstetrician arrived about five hours later, performed the C-section, and delivered the baby, who by that time was severely brain-damaged. He offered no excuse or apology to the parents.

The child is now in a special school and requires almost constant care and attention. When one considers the millions of dollars in medical, education, and other costs that this family will incur over the life of this child, the settlement is not as much as it seems. This boy and his family will have to live with pain for the rest of their lives. The verdict, however, will at least prevent them from having to worry about how they are going to pay the extraordinary bills. In that respect, the family was more fortunate that many others. A 1992 study by Vanderbilt University, of patients who sued their doctors after incurring serious injuries, found that when the costs of the injury, treatment, and lost earnings are factored in, these patients received an average of only about 60 percent of what the injuries actually cost them.

The AMA and others miss the point when they argue that the current system of malpractice litigation doesn't work, that awards have grown too high, and that they don't bear any relation to the costs associated with the injuries received. The AMA paints a picture of juries that are fooled by sharp lawyers into granting big judgments to undeserving plaintiffs. But juries are smarter than that.

When a baby is born brain-damaged because the doctor didn't show up in the labor room to notice that the fetus was in distress, when a doctor ignores a woman's breast cancer until it's too late, when a physician's blatant neglect or incompetence causes the needless death of a patient, juries are outraged. They want to make sure that the plaintiff is properly compensated, and they grant awards that they hope will both provide that compensation and send a message to doctors that such behavior is not going to be tolerated.

According to a study conducted for the Rand Corporation and others, reported in the *New England Journal of Medicine,* June 8, 1974,

> Damages awarded in a malpractice suit must be viewed not only as compensating the victim but also as deterring health-care providers from negligent behavior. . . . The negligence system makes a great deal more sense if it is understood primarily as a means to deter careless behavior rather than to compensate its victims. By finding fault and assessing damages against the negligent provider, the system sends all providers a signal that discourages future carelessness and reduces future damages.

In the *Gonzalez* v. *Nork* case in California (mentioned in chapter 5), the judge ruled that the need for deterrence is obvious because of the failure of the medical profession to discipline itself. He went on to point out that malpractice litigation had actually been beneficial to the medical profession, highlighting areas in which performance needed to be improved.

The Rand Corporation study went on to note that some observers feel juries should not be allowed to consider a plaintiff's pain and suffering in contemplating the amount of award: "But someone whose injury affects his life-style—say the ability to participate in recreation or the ability to have children—is paying a price that is properly included in a damages award. . . . The effect on life-style is enormous and a jury properly assesses the loss as a real injury that can only be compensated monetarily. In these terms, even the largest awards do not seem excessive."

Virtually every objective investigation of the medical malpractice crisis in America has shown conclusively that the cause of the crisis is not the lawsuits but the malpractice. A U.S. Senate Subcommittee found more than twenty years ago that "most malpractice suits are the direct result of injuries suffered by patients during medical treatment or surgery. The majority have proved justifiable."

According to testimony by Sidney M. Wolfe, M.D., before the Senate Health Subcommittee on May 7, 1986, "the genesis of the malpractice problem was not thought to be in the legal or insurance professions but, rather, in medicine itself. Something is wrong with the *quality* of health care in this country." And a former director of the federal government's Commission on Medical Malpractice, Eli Hernzweig, has commented that "the time has come for all parties seeking solutions to malpractice problems to recognize that the root cause of the current malpractice problem is the substantial number of injuries and other adverse results sustained by patients during the course of hospital and medical treatment."

The medical community and the insurance industry continue working in Washington and in state capitals to persuade America that malpractice lawsuits represent a public policy crisis. Their contentions are baloney from start to finish. But since the medical and insurance industries contributed more than $10 million to U.S. House and Senate candidates for the 1992 elections—not to mention millions more to state legislators around the country— they have access to the corridors of power. And since physicians are generally revered by most of the American public, these lobbyists have a receptive audience for their message.

As a result, rather than cracking down on incompetent doctors, there are moves afoot to place the public at even greater risk and deny the victimized an opportunity to seek justice. Rather than take steps to protect patients, these groups seek to limit lawsuits against negligent doctors and enact various types of tort reform legislation. Though they don't admit it, tort reform would, in essence, lock the public out of the courtroom and limit the recourse available to injured people. Tort reform plans come in many different names—caps on awards, no-fault, arbitration—all of which sound perfectly reasonable. Proponents claim that these plans would benefit the public, that they would provide compensation to greater numbers of injured people. If you cap awards, they say, you can prevent an overly emotional jury from imposing an unfairly high judgment that drives up insurance premiums.

Arbitration, they say, would make it easier for patients to have access to the legal system. They would no longer need to hire a lawyer and go through the courts.

Presumably, a no-fault system would make sure that those who suffer injuries would be compensated. Since individual doctors would no longer be sued, and a doctor's liability would no longer be an issue, there would be no cover-ups of negligence and, while no one would be able to get the type of large awards they are sometimes able to obtain at present, everyone would receive some compensation.

That's what the AMA says. That's what the insurance companies say. The fact is, however, that these tort reform measures have four things in common: The insurance companies save money. Incompetent doctors avoid blame and any meaningful form of discipline. Patients and their families, who have been destroyed in the process, are prevented from obtaining the only kind of justice available to them, financial compensation. And the public is left unprotected from doctors who maim and kill their patients.

Presumably, the AMA believes that if patients who are victims of medical incompetence don't sue, or don't receive large awards for their suffering, then doctors won't have to pay as much for insurance. They are engaging in a big lie strategy to achieve passage of tort reform that would undoubtedly reduce insurance costs—not by lessening the occurrence of malpractice but by reducing the penalties and immunizing physicians from liability.

Various tort reform measures have made their way through the legislatures in a number of states. California has put limits on the amount of money plaintiffs can receive for noneconomic damages, like pain and suffering. New York allows awards of more than $250,000 to be paid out to the plaintiff over a number of years, rather than in one lump sum, as is usually the custom. At the time of this writing, Vermont is considering legislation to replace the court system for trying malpractice cases with a dispute resolution system, or some form of arbitration. Illinois is considering establishing a screening panel whose rulings could require plaintiffs, if they lose the case, to pay the court costs of their opponents. It would also prohibit juries from assessing punitive damages against malpracticing doctors and would allow for installment payments of large awards.

Perhaps the most damaging assault has come from the White House and Congress, both of which are considering legislation that would force states to institute changes in the way medical malpractice cases are resolved. In the last year of his administration, President Bush proposed legislation designed to encourage states to place caps on noneconomic damages; limit joint and several liability, which allows patients to sue several parties (the doctor, the hospital, the anesthesiologist if they were all partly responsible for the malpractice); allow the payment of large awards in installments; and spur development of alternative dispute resolution, arbitration, no-fault, or other methods of resolving claims out of court. It is not yet clear how President Clinton will deal with these issues as he advances his health-care agenda. But members of his staff have already suggested that the legislation he proposes should contain measures to limit malpractice litigation against doctors—a step that could mirror the proposals of the previous administration.

What's wrong with these initiatives? Let's take them one at a time.

Alternative dispute resolution often means a no-fault system similar to workers' compensation. Under such a system, everyone who was injured by a doctor would receive compensation without going to court. There would be no findings of liability or guilt against doctors. Long and costly court proceedings would be eliminated and patients who are injured would generally receive fairly small awards.

The Commonwealth of Virginia instituted a no-fault system in 1988 to deal solely with cases of brain-damaged children. The theory in no-fault is that if doctors don't have to admit their mistakes publicly (thus the term *no-fault*), more cases of malpractice will come to light and more of these unfortunate children and their families will benefit. For the first five years of this program, from January 1, 1988, to January 1, 1993, not one single award was made to a brain-damaged child or its parents in Virginia. Then in early 1993, the Virginia Attorney General's office reported that they had made three awards, for a paltry total of $65,000, less than $22,000 per brain-damaged child.

Even under a relatively effective no-fault system, the benefits are only theoretical. Because doctors would have to be sufficiently insured to be covered for injuries that are not necessarily the result of negligence as well as those that are, a far greater number of claims would have to be paid. And insurance premiums would reflect that. Neither would no-fault serve the intended purpose of entirely eliminating lawsuits. There would always be disputes, for example, just as there are under workers' compensation or under the no-fault systems of automobile insurance. According to the Rand Corporation report, "the combined cost of such litigation, and of payments to patients who were injured but not as a result of negligence, could well offset the overall savings that a no-fault system might otherwise achieve."

In addition, by eliminating the standard of fault, any deterrent effect that malpractice lawsuits now have on incompetent doctors would also be eliminated. "What we need," as Public Citizen's Dr. Sidney Wolfe has noted, "is more fault, not no fault." "Replacing the present tort system with a no-fault insurance scheme would not necessarily be cheaper," according to the Rand Report, and "it might well abolish the deterrent signal or distort clinical decision making."

Other alternative dispute mechanisms frequently discussed involve either substituting or supplementing juries with panels of "experts," who presumably are better able to understand the complicated facts of a malpractice case than laypeople. Such panels might be part of an arbitration process that takes the place of a trial by jury. Or they might be screening panels that rule on the merits of cases before they go to trial. The theory is that juries lack the ability to form intelligent opinions on such complicated matters, and thus make emotional decisions and give unreasonably high awards to plaintiffs.

In other words, proponents of tort reform feel that juries, which are perfectly capable of ruling on whether to send a murderer to the electric chair, are not competent to rule fairly and impartially when a physician is accused of malpractice. Eliminating trials by jury singles out the medical profession for protection against lawsuits that is not afforded to any other profession in this country.

A variation of the panel system is one in which, even if the panel decides against the plaintiff, he or she can still proceed with the lawsuit. The rationale is that the panel, under these circumstances, does not deny victims their right to a trial by jury. It simply deters plaintiffs from pursuing frivolous lawsuits. In effect, however, this stage adds to the cost and time of the process, thus deterring meritorious lawsuits as well as frivolous ones.

Under some panel proposals, if the panel rules against the plaintiff and he or she proceeds to trial anyway, the plaintiff would have to pay the doctor's legal bills if the lawsuit fails. Such a system just adds insult to injury. Unless you have financial resources to begin with, you have to be absolutely sure you are going to win before you even start a legal action. There are never any such guarantees. Many people, particularly the poor, are already injured and in debt as a result of their medical bills and will decline to pursue legal action for fear of losing and owing even more money. The *New York Times* editorialized on February 15, 1992, that "supporters of the 'loser pays' rule believe it discourages frivolous lawsuits. It also discourages legitimate but risky ones. Similar arguments apply to contingency-fee arrangements by which lawyers get a percentage of the winnings, but only if they win. Such fees often provide the only access to justice for people without means."

Another often-discussed proposal would place limits on the amount of money a patient could receive for noneconomic damages such as pain and suffering, emotional distress, disfigurement, and loss of companionship. Proponents argue that when someone has been injured or killed as a result of medical incompetence, the compensation that the individual or family receives should reflect only whatever economic loss has been suffered. The injured party should be compensated for such things as medical bills and lost wages, but should not become eligible for a windfall at the expense of the doctor and the insurance company.

Harriet Hamlin would probably disagree. This fifty-four-year-old woman is the owner of a successful neighborhood bar, and she was used to dealing with all types of people and all sorts of problems. In 1972, she was diagnosed as having lupus, a disease that shows up as blotches on the skin and often leads to lung and respiratory problems. It can also sometimes cause vascular disease, affecting circulation in certain blood vessels. Unfazed, Ms. Hamlin went about her life, running her business, enjoying the regular company of the people who were both friends and patrons of her establishment.

In 1981, she discovered she had lung cancer, but she fought back, and after a part of her lung was removed, she continued working full time, with the exception of certain days on which her chemotherapy left her feeling ill.

In February 1988, she began complaining to her family physician, Dr. Sam Lipkin, of a shortness of breath and some difficulty walking. She continued seeing Dr. Lipkin regularly over the next seven months, during which time cramps in her big toe and right foot got continually worse until she told the doctor she could hardly walk. Dr. Lipkin diagnosed her as having a blood disorder related to her lupus, and had her admitted to the hospital for a series of blood transfusions.

While at the hospital a bone-marrow test was done to determine whether she was suffering from leukemia. The results were negative. Her only problem was the blood disorder, which she was told was causing anemia and her other problems. During her hospital stay, blood tests, CAT scans, and X-rays all were said to be negative.

After being released from the hospital in October, Ms. Hamlin began seeing a hemotologist, Dr. Raymond Polonavitz, every two weeks on an outpatient basis. During the next two months, under Dr. Polonavitz's care, her right foot turned blue and she began feeling tingling, numbness, and occasional pain in her left foot. In January 1989, he referred her to a surgeon, Dr. Richard Vassal, for further examination. Dr. Vassal wrote a letter back to Dr. Polonavitz saying that he did not believe that Ms. Hamlin's problem had anything to do with lupus, as Drs. Lipkin and Polonavitz had been assuming. He did not believe it had anything to do with a blood disorder. He believed she had emboli, or blood clots, impairing the flow of blood in her legs. He recommended an aortogram and angiogram—tests to determine whether the emboli existed. Dr. Polonovitz received this letter, but never told his patient about it.

At the end of February—more than a year after Ms. Hamlin began complaining to Dr. Lipkin of pain in her foot and difficulty walking, four months after first meeting Dr. Polonavitz in the hospital—she finally went on her own to the emergency room. The emergency room resident examined her and noted that there was no pulse in her lower legs, her feet were white, and her toes were blue. The exploratory tests that Dr. Vassal had recommended a month earlier were now performed. Indeed, there were blockages of arteries in both legs. Emergency surgery was performed to remove the blood clots. The following day the circulation in her legs had not returned. More surgery was done, but to no avail. A week later, both of her legs—now gangrenous—were amputated just below the knee.

A succession of doctors, each relying on mistaken diagnoses, had allowed Ms. Hamlin's legs to be slowly destroyed over a period of thirteen months. She followed their medical advice to the letter. She went for her regular schedule of examinations, and when they mistakenly attributed her vascular problems to a blood disorder, she went to the hospital for her transfusions. During all this time no one thought that a middle-aged patient, complaining of pain and numbness in her toes, might have a circulatory problem—might have blocked blood vessels that need to be cleared or repaired— even though she had been suffering for seventeen years with a disease, lupus, that sometimes causes precisely that type of problem. When one doctor did suspect the true problem, his advice was ignored, delaying her treatment for an additional month.

A lawsuit in this case has now been filed, but the outcome will not be determined for some time. Ms. Hamlin still owns her bar, but she is not able to get there very often. She has lost touch with most of her old friends and customers. She is now separated from her husband, and faces years of painful and costly physical rehabilitation. Worst of all, this vital, gregarious woman must now face all this alone.

The AMA and other tort-reform advocates should ask Ms. Hamlin about pain and suffering, emotional distress, disfigurement, and loss of companionship. They should explain to her why a limitation should be placed on the amount of money she can receive as a result of the malpractice committed against her. These types of caps are not in Ms. Hamlin's interest. They are not just, and they do not represent the way the American legal system should work.

Indiana is one state whose laws include both caps on awards and panels to screen cases before they go to trial. Physicians' groups said the Indiana law was a model for national reform when it was passed in 1975. But according to the *Indianapolis Star* (June 26,

1990), "the act has turned out to benefit the two groups who lobbied hardest for its passage—doctors and their insurance companies—far more than it benefits malpractice victims and their families."

Indiana caps awards of any kind at $750,000, an amount that does not begin to compensate for the costs that can be incurred by many victims of malpractice. A young child, for example, severely injured or brain-damaged at birth, will have millions of dollars of expenses during his life. And verdicts that may seem large by today's standards may turn out to be inadequate decades into the future, when inflation has reduced the value of the dollar. Fifty years ago, for example, a $50,000 award for a brain-damaged child might have seemed like a lot of money. But it would hardly be sufficient today to meet the needs of that same victim, now grown to adulthood.

Who ends up paying when awards are capped? Few malpractice victims can afford to do it on their own. If the legal system has not provided adequate means—or if caps on awards have prevented them from receiving what they deserve—the government ends up paying the difference, usually in the form of Medicaid or other programs that pay for health care and various services for the disabled. Is that a fair system? The taxpayers foot the bill while the guilty physician and his insurance company get off by paying only a fraction of the true cost of the negligence.

Neither has the panel system proved a great success in Indiana. The panels, which render nonbinding opinions on cases before they go to trial, were supposed to speed the process. But with a backlog of 1,200 cases, it takes almost three years to get a panel decision—three years before the trial process can even start.

These panels rarely work in favor of the victims of malpractice, but in Indiana, where the panels consist of three doctors, they rule against patients most of the time. This trend may be explained by the *Indianapolis Star*'s finding that more than one-quarter of these panels include at least one doctor who has, himself, been sued for malpractice.

Critics of the Indiana law point out that, while its objectives were to attract more doctors to the state and to reduce the cost of

health care, it has accomplished neither. Indiana still has the sev-
enth-lowest number of doctors per capita of any state in the country, and the cost of a hospital stay is still higher than in many states
that have not enacted this type of tort reform.

Again, it seems clear, not only from logical assumptions based
on our own experience but from information in states where tort
reform has been enacted, that these "reforms" do nothing to benefit the American public. Despite this evidence, however, the campaign for tort reform continues.

Another proposal that has been bandied about would either limit
or eliminate the concept of joint and several liability. Many of the
cases we've described in this book illustrate this concept. For
example, consider the case of an obstetrician who fails to arrive to
examine his patient when she goes into labor, and when fetal distress occurs, the child is brain-damaged. In such a case, several
parties might share liability: the obstetrician, for not showing up;
the hospital, for failing to act in the doctor's absence when fetal
distress occurred; and probably other physicians as well—the hospital resident, the anesthesiologist—who were present and
neglected to provide the care necessary to save the baby.

What if it turns out that the obstetrician has no malpractice
insurance? Or only a small policy that will be insufficient to compensate his victim? Under joint and several liability, the other doctors and the hospital would all be held liable for paying whatever
amount the jury awarded. That is the best system for ensuring that
patients receive the awards they are entitled to. After all, if the
obstetrician's negligence includes the failure to maintain an adequate insurance policy, the victim should not have to suffer
twice—once because of malpractice and again from failure to collect the judgment.

The tort reformers say that the defendants in a malpractice lawsuit should be responsible for paying damages only in direct proportion to the degree of their liability. If the jury finds the
obstetrician 60 percent liable, the hospital 30 percent liable, and
the resident and anesthesiologist each 5 percent liable, then each

would be responsible for paying only that percentage of the award. If the obstetrician has no insurance, the plaintiff loses 60 percent of the award. The insurance companies are protected, and the child's family is left to figure out how best to pay a lifetime of bills.

Another popular proposal would allow doctors who have been found guilty of negligence and their insurance companies to pay out large awards over a period of time. The logic of this proposal is that, usually, a large part of the award in a malpractice case is to cover the cost of future medical expenses and the loss of future earnings. Since those expenses occur over time, why require payment in one lump sum, right after the judgment is rendered?

First is the issue of fairness. The victim of malpractice should have control over the full amount of the award, to spend as he or she deems fit. A disabled person may want to spend a large amount of money immediately to purchase a specially designed house to accommodate the handicap. The family of an injured child may want to travel to another city to consult with other physicians. Another family might want to invest the money and use it later on for the child's education. After going through the trauma of medical negligence and years of litigation to prove it, the plaintiff should be entitled to that freedom. He or she should not have to go back into court each time there is an unusual expenditure or ask permission from the doctor or insurance company.

In addition, if the defendant can hold on to that money and pay it out in installments, then he or she will be able to invest it and keep the earnings on money that rightly belongs to the plaintiff. If the award is paid in a lump sum, the malpractice victim can invest that money and the award then increases in value. As we have seen, insurance companies are already making tremendous profits in this area. They should not be allowed to make more at the expense of people who are proven victims of negligence.

Tort-reform advocates have been successful in a number of states, and usually the results for the public have been negative. Six years ago, for example, in response to rising insurance costs and what was thought to be a litigation crisis, Colorado enacted a comprehensive tort-reform package containing many of the measures discussed here, but covering all types of litigation, not just medical malpractice. According to the March 3, 1992, *Wall Street Journal,*

> Commercial insurance premiums have gone down much less than the business community anticipated. Auto insurance, the major insurance cost for consumers, is actually more expensive than it was before the legal reforms were passed.
>
> Frivolous suits are less likely to reap big awards, but so are lawsuits that nearly anyone would consider valid. Cases involving catastrophic injury to the plaintiff and egregious wrongdoing by the defendant are highlighting the flip side of reform: The most seriously hurt are the most likely to see their damages reduced the most under the new laws. . . . The overall impact on the insurance policyholder has not been great. The insurers have benefited more than individual customers. . . .

The restrictive Colorado laws seem to be a failure by any measure. The most important thing these reforms were supposed to accomplish was a reduction in litigation, but since their enactment, the number of lawsuits has actually increased.

Colorado is now considering repealing some of those laws, but its experience is well worth examining. So are the ethical sensibilities of public officials who are so easily led by lobbyists into a mindset that blames the injured, the disabled, and the victims of medical ineptitude and neglect.

These "reforms"—purportedly advanced in the public interest—are actually in the interests of no one but the thousands of physicians who will be allowed to practice bad medicine undetected, undeterred, and untroubled by their conscience or the courts.

8

CAREFUL PATIENTS— GOOD DOCTORS

In this book we have described numerous horror stories about medical mishaps and injuries. Having thus warned about the significant amount of negligence and malpractice that occurs in our nation's hospitals, clinics, and doctors' offices, we may have left the impression that people should stay out of the hands of physicians at all cost. That is not the message we intend.

Our message is that while patients often need the services of physicians, they should not place their faith in them blindly. Most physicians are excellent. Modern medicine can, when practiced properly, benefit patients enormously. But physicians need to take more time with their patients and provide better care. And patients need to be better prepared, better informed, and more active participants in their own health-care decisions.

If the public is to be protected against malpractice, its best chance is to protect itself. The evidence shows that, at the present time, there is no other meaningful protection available against even the worst members of the medical profession. There is no system that cracks down on even the most inadequate hospitals and health-care institutions. Some physicians give the impression that they are more concerned with protecting their colleagues than protecting the public. Medical societies close their eyes to the problem. The state licensing boards that are supposed to discipline negligent physicians just don't do the job.

Obviously, it is impossible to provide an absolute, foolproof guide that, in ten easy steps, would protect patients from becoming victims of malpractice. However, there are certain actions patients can take to improve their odds and minimize their risks. In fact, this advice—based on common problems that arise in most of our malpractice cases as well as our medical and legal training—is meant for physicians as much as for patients. By making relatively small changes in the way they deal with the public, doctors can minimize their risks as well.

We have explained throughout this book the need for a change in attitude among the medical profession, and we will discuss that further a little later on. But what is also crucial is a change in patient attitudes. Patients need to begin expecting as high a level of accountability of their physicians as they do of any other service provider. Generally speaking, Americans are among the most discerning consumers in the world. Now they need to become just as demanding in their medical care.

Since its inception, the medical profession has seemed mysterious to most laypeople. In much the same way that practitioners in ancient times kept their cures and treatments shrouded in secrecy, doctors today rarely see the need to discuss their methods with patients. All too often they think—and sometimes tell their patients—that medical procedures are too complicated for laypeople to understand.

Competent members of the medical profession certainly deserve our respect, but doctors are no more entitled to this mystique than practitioners of other complex professions. The American public is capable of buying hi-tech computer equipment, spending billions of dollars on complex machinery for the home or office. Most of us would not be able to build a computer; most computer owners probably do not even know what exactly makes the machine work. Yet we comparison shop, do our homework, learn about warranties and reliability, then try out different models before we make the purchase. How many people give that amount of thought to their physician? We would never buy a computer from a salesperson who wouldn't spend time with us, wouldn't answer our questions, wouldn't deal directly with our complaints. Why should we accept that behavior from the individuals from whom we purchase our medical services?

"Health-care experts say there is much that patients can do to protect themselves against incompetent and negligent medical care," said the *New York Times* (January 30, 1976):

> The average health-care consumer is often too poorly informed and too easily intimidated to select, judge and demand the kind of care every patient deserves, these experts contend. Consumer education in the health field, they say, would result in patients' gaining better care for themselves and their families and provide the fastest and surest means of eliminating incompetent medical practices and practitioners.
>
> An informed health-care consumer knows how and when to choose his doctors and what questions to ask to assure adequate preventive care and proper diagnosis and treatment of an illness. He knows what to tell the doctor about himself, how to identify a good hospital, how to find out if surgery is needed and how generally to act in his own interests as a patient.
>
> The choice of a physician can be a life and death decision. Yet many doctors believe that people often choose a new car more carefully than they choose a doctor.

Notice the use of the term *health-care consumer.* It is vital that people begin viewing themselves in this way—as consumers, entitled to the same rights that consumers normally enjoy. And they should make the effort to learn how to become prudent health-care consumers.

The first step comes in the selection of a doctor. Whether it be a general practitioner or a specialist, patients should shop around for the best individual available. This may sound like an obvious point, but many people choose doctors for all the wrong reasons. They select someone because he is located near their home, or because a neighbor uses him, or because they heard his name on a radio talk show. These are not good indicators of a physician's competence. Others choose a physician because he or she is of the same religion or practices at a religiously affiliated institution. Still others choose the doctor who charges the lowest fee, or accepts assignment from their health insurance plan (so that they don't have to incur any out-of-pocket expenses). Occasionally, patients select a doctor's name out of the Yellow Pages.

Wanting to watch expenses is understandable, but often, as the proverb goes, this approach is penny wise and pound foolish. Obviously, some people have no choice but to make decisions based on cost. But for many others, attempts to save a few dollars come at the expense of good medical care. If a physician is chosen simply because he accepts assignment from the patient's insurance, and during his examination he overlooks the patient's early stage cancer, what has the patient really saved? The price of that examination may cost the patient his life.

Likewise, the publicity a doctor receives and such extraneous factors as religious affiliation are no reflection of medical ability. Bad doctors come from every religion, and they often get a lot of good publicity.

Also, while it certainly is most convenient to use those physicians and hospitals that are closest to home, these might not be the most effective people or locations at which to be treated. Compared to the inconvenience of being a malpractice victim, traveling across town to the best doctor available is a small matter. Patients should take the trouble to protect themselves by getting the best care possible.

Consumers should also be cautious about physician referral services, many of which claim to check the credentials of the doctors they list. In fact, most of these services are based on financial arrangements between the physician and service, not necessarily on physician competence. Even referrals by hospitals should be questioned. Community-based hospitals usually have on staff those physicians who are geographically close to the facility, and there is no assurance that their credentials and expertise have been verified.

It is easy to make a mistake in choosing a doctor; it usually cannot be done with just one phone call. If possible, it is always best to select a physician when reasonably healthy, since it requires some effort. But even when under the strain of an illness—perhaps especially then—patients need to do some homework. If the patient is unable to do it for himself, perhaps he will be fortunate enough to have a friend or family member who can help. Given the importance that selection of a physician has, it should certainly not be taken lightly.

One way to start is by asking for recommendations from physicians you know to be competent, who will usually refer patients to other competent physicians. Occasionally, however, doctors may refer colleagues with whom they socialize, or who refer patients to them, rather than on an objective appraisal of their competence. Then prospective patients need to take these referrals a few steps further.

Ask about credentials. It is usually best if the physician you choose is a graduate of an accredited U.S. medical school. As we'll discuss in a moment, the country in which a doctor receives medical education can make a tremendous difference.

Ask where the doctor did his or her residency and whether he or she is board certified in the particular area of practice. To be board certified, physicians must do their residency in approved programs, and pass rigorous exams during their residency and then again two years into their practice. There is a board for virtually every medical specialty, and board certification is a mark of competence that every doctor wants to obtain.

It is also important to know what hospitals or universities the physician is affiliated with. An affiliation with a large medical center, or teaching or university hospital, is an important credential, and it is sometimes best to avoid physicians who lack it. Medicine is an ever-changing science, with new advances, new treatments, and new research being done every day. Doctors who are active in a university environment or who work at a prestigious research facility are most likely to keep abreast of latest developments—and the latest trouble spots.

Also, these institutions usually are home to the most advanced diagnostic and treatment technologies—all of which patients want at their disposal if the need arises. All too often patients suffer because a hospital lacks adequate equipment and there is a delay in transfering them to other facilities.

A physician's educational background is extremely important. Not only are most states lax in disciplining doctors who commit malpractice, they are surprisingly lenient in screening medical school graduates who apply for licenses. Most states allow candidates to take the licensing exam several times; in other words, if they fail the test they can take it again—and again and again—until they pass.

American medical schools are probably the finest in the world, and most graduates are among the brightest young men and women in our country. But there are currently about 25,000 doctors practicing in the United States who not only didn't graduate from these schools, but couldn't even get admitted to them. Many of these 25,000 individuals were rejected by American medical schools and received their education in substandard schools in Mexico and the Caribbean.

Juliet Marco, a sixty-five-year-old Pennsylvania woman, had a history of heart problems and was taking medication for an arrhythmia, or irregular heart beat. She had recently been diagnosed as having a fibroid tumor, which her physician told her would require a total hysterectomy. This advice was wrong from the start—another example of unnecessary surgery. Ms. Marco was in no danger. There was no reason for surgery to be performed except to allow the doctors involved to collect on the patient's medical insurance. A fibroid tumor is not malignant and posed no threat to her life. She had no serious symptoms—no bleeding, no anemia—that indicated a need for surgery. According to two sonograms taken two years apart, the tumor had not enlarged. In a woman her age, postmenopausal, the tumor probably would have shrunk over time on its own. On the other hand, major abdominal surgery on a patient with a history of heart ailments is a significant risk—a risk that in this case should have been avoided.

As it happened, on the very day Juliet Marco was scheduled for surgery, she appeared at the hospital emergency room complaining of palpitations, chest tightness, and shortness of breath. Apparently she had run out of heart medication and had not taken any for about two days. Her heart rate was 180 and her blood pressure had dropped significantly. The emergency room staff put her on an intravenous antiarrhythmic drug, which seemed to improve her condition. She was transferred from the emergency room to the main hospital.

That afternoon, her doctor reviewed the record of her emergency room visit. Even if her previous history had not been sufficient to prevent this individual from recommending surgery, one would think that the patient's crisis—occurring on that same day—would haved dissuaded him. Just consider this woman's condition: That morning, her heart rate had been 180, her blood pressure had been extremely low, and emergency treatment had been needed to stabilize her. Add to that another complication—the hospital had run out of her type of blood. Surgery under these circumstances should have been inconceivable. Nevertheless, her physician decided to proceed with the hysterectomy the following morning.

During the surgery Ms. Marco lost a lot of blood, placing a great strain on her heart. Almost immediately after surgery she went into cardiac arrest and stopped breathing. She was resuscitated and kept alive in a vegetative state, with significant brain damage. While in this coma she developed pulmonary emboli—blood clots—and a device was inserted in her vein to allow the blood to flow while preventing the clots from traveling to the heart and lung. But the device came loose and moved through a major vein to her heart, requiring open heart surgery to remove it. Finally, after three months, a second cardiac arrest ended Ms. Marco's life. Her hospital bill, at the conclusion of her "treatment," was in excess of $265,000.

When we looked into this case, we found that the physician responsible for Ms. Marco undergoing the initial surgery, which unnecessarily cost the patient her life, had received his degree from a medical school in Ensenada, Mexico.

A television network news program became interested in the Marco matter and began an investigation into the entire subject of foreign-educated doctors practicing in the United States. The network sent a reporter undercover to the school where Ms. Marco's doctor was educated—one of a number of schools that accept and train American medical-school rejects. The reporter, posing as an applicant for admission, told the head of this institution that he had never graduated from college and did not speak Spanish—something he thought would be a handicap, given that many of the courses were taught in Spanish. No problem, he was told. After an interview lasting just a few minutes, he was accepted as a student.

What the reporter found during his stay there was a medical library about the size of a bathroom with a few out-of-date publications, and a laboratory that looked less equipped than most high school labs. In a typical American medical school, students spend a great deal of time practicing on and learning anatomy from human cadavers. Here there were no cadavers. Students said that the school did have a cadaver once. Apparently the body of a Russian sailor washed up on the beach, and they were able to use it for a time, but they soon realized that, after soaking in the ocean and then left unrefrigerated at the school, the body had worms and was unusable.

Students at this school—who qualify for student loans backed by the U.S. government—talked openly about how anyone, even the "dumbest people," could obtain medical degrees there. One young man said he wasn't worried about the low quality of his training—that he would learn on the job. "This is like driver's training," he said. "You never really learn how to drive until [you] actually have your license already and [are] driving your car."

These are people who will be practicing medicine in this country in a few years. Frightening, isn't it? All these students have to do to be eligible to practice medicine in the United States is to pass a multiple-choice test. They are allowed to continue taking the test, no matter how many times they fail, until they receive a passing grade. At this point, they can qualify to take the appropriate state-licensing exams.

So, clearly this is an area that consumers should look into and be concerned about. Some foreign medical schools, particularly in some European countries, are excellent. But those in the Caribbean and Mexico that accept American medical-school rejects are nothing more than diploma mills. So when you see those impressive-looking diplomas hanging on a doctor's wall, don't just admire them from afar. Get up close and read them. If they are from one of these substandard institutions, you might want to look for another doctor.

Much information on doctors can be obtained prior to a visit to the doctor's office. Sometimes the physician's office assistant or receptionist will answer questions over the phone. If not, reference books such as *Who's Who in Medical Specialties*, the *Directory of Medical Specialists*, or the *American Medical Association Directory*, which provide brief descriptions of most physicians' credentials, are in the reference section of most public libraries. These books are very easy to use. They are updated periodically, and new editions are usually published every year or two.

While at the library, people can avail themselves of another source of physicians' names by doing a computer search of professional literature on the particular disease or area of interest. Most libraries can arrange such searches, which provide, by topic, a list of articles and studies that have been published in medical journals. One way to determine who the leaders are in a particular field is to go through these articles and identify the physicians who have written or done research on them. These physicians might take on private patients themselves, or would certainly be a good source for referrals.

In addition, this particular exercise can pay off in other ways. Not only will consumers be able to learn about leaders in the medical field of interest, but reading the articles and scrutinizing the research will provide information that may be useful later. Patients who are knowledgeable about their condition are best able to provide pertinent information to their doctors and to ask the educated, intelligent questions that will help ensure they receive the best treatment possible.

Another important piece of information patients should have is whether the doctor they are considering has a history of disciplinary actions or malpractice judgments. As we have seen, this may be difficult to ascertain, but state health departments usually inform people who inquire if a specific doctor has been disciplined. Procedures for obtaining this information vary from state to state, and often involve the frustrating experience of being transferred from office to office in search of the bureaucrat who can provide it. And the answer will hardly be definitive, with most states acting on only a small percentage of the complaints they receive and disciplining only a fraction of the incompetent doctors. Still, it's important to check. If your doctor has had his or her license suspended or been disciplined in any other way, you ought to know about it.

Another source of bad doctors' names is the Public Citizen Health Research Group in Washington, D.C., which each year publishes a list of thousands of doctors around the country who have committed various offenses. Although it only scratches the surface, it is one of the few attempts being made to inform the public about incompetent physicians.

One mistake many people make is to wait until they are sick—and under obvious pressure—before thinking about their medical care. Many people don't even have a family doctor—the internist or general practitioner who gives the check-up and treats minor ailments. Having a family doctor, however, is highly advisable. This physician can become a repository of information about a patient's medical history—information that may be vital to forming an accurate diagnosis in cases of serious illness later on. The physician can also use what he or she knows about a patient's background for references to appropriate specialists. For example, if a patient develops circulatory problems in his foot, it might be important, before referring him to a vascular surgeon, to know that he has diabetes. And as the vascular surgeon develops a course of treatment, it will be important for him or her to know what medication the patient has been on and various other aspects of his history over time. It is useful to have one individual who can provide all that information, and who can offer advice and insight on whatever specialists the patient might need.

Among the most important things prospective patients should keep in mind are the principal failings we've already detailed that lead to most incidents of malpractice: failure of the physician to be present when needed, failure to perform an adequate examination, and failure to take a thorough medical history. People should choose physicians who they believe are going to avoid these three basic pitfalls.

If a physician is a solo practitioner, find out how to contact him or her after hours in case of emergency. How difficult is the doctor to reach by phone, during office hours and after? What happens when she is on vacation? Does she have someone else cover for her at times? If so, what are that person's credentials? The worst thing that can happen is to diligently research a physician's background and then, when a crisis comes, have your call answered by another physician who is totally unfamiliar.

These issues are particularly important when selecting an obstetrician or pediatrician. Many problems develop in the labor room that can be disastrous for both mother and child. A competent, board-certified obstetrician must be present in the labor room, no matter what time of day it is. Expectant parents should question prospective obstetricians carefully on this point and not select one unless they are sure he will be there when they need him—or can provide a qualified substitute in the event it is necessary.

Likewise, the selection of a pediatrician to care for the child after birth is difficult as well. Children get sick at all hours, and a pediatrician who is difficult to reach during the evening or on weekends is of limited use. So is the pediatrician who routinely diagnoses sick children over the phone, always assuming that "it's just some bug going around," rather than examining the child. Never accept a pediatrician who seems reluctant to give credence to your concerns or to inconvenience him or herself at odd hours. We have seen too many cases where young children have had high fevers and their doctors—rather than interrupt their weekend—decided after speaking with the mother on the phone that it was nothing. Later on, what they lazily assumed was a "bug" actually was meningitis or some other serious illness that needs immediate attention and treatment.

Sometimes, good group practices are a way of avoiding problems like these. In group practices, several physicians work together and one of them is always on call. Patients know in advance who all of their doctor's partners are and have an opportunity to meet them and check on their credentials and qualifications. Patients can be assured that even if the primary physician is not available for some reason, there will be another doctor—one they know they can trust—whom they can see if they need to. An added benefit is the ease with which these physicians consult each other on difficult cases, thus providing an additional measure of protection for the patient.

Regrettably, even physicians with good credentials—even those who are on call when needed—don't always practice good medicine. Patients also need to judge the doctor by his or her behavior during the initial office visit and in subsequent visits.

One of the first things that should happen at that first visit is the compilation of a thorough medical history of the patient, without which a physical examination is nothing more than a mechanical process. Rather than simply jumping to conclusions as some physicians do, doctors should take their time, letting the patient tell his or her story in as much detail as it takes. The history should include everything in the patient's life that has been medically relevant up to the point of consulting with this physician—obviously with an emphasis on whatever the problem at hand happens to be. Of course, most patients are not able to provide this kind of revealing history unaided. The physician needs to help them—to ask questions, to search out relevant details. For example, patients may refer to themselves as tense or anxious—conditions that are hard to define—or they may use terms like *cold, flu,* or *virus* to describe a wide variety of ailments. A patient may say he is short of breath, leading the doctor in one direction, when actually he is only breathing shallowly because of pain caused by something entirely different. Therefore, it is important for the physician to get the whole story. The patient is not always the best diagnostician—that's the doctor's job. And although medical authorities uniformly agree that taking a medical history is one of a doctor's most important tasks, a surprising number of doctors have shortcomings in this area.

In taking the history, the doctor should review in detail (in addition to the patient's current complaints) such things as:

- Past illnesses, injuries, and hospitalizations;
- marital status, health of partner, number and ages of children;
- whether the patient takes medications, smokes, or drinks;
- whether the patient's occupation involves any stress or hazard;
- family history of diseases like diabetes, hypertension, and cancer;
- whether the patient suffers from headaches or has any vision, hearing, or respiratory problems;
- any symptoms, such as shortness of breath, palpitations, or leg cramps, that might indicate cardiovascular problems;
- description of the patient's appetite, the presence of nausea or vomiting, changes in the form of stool or urination;
- significant changes in the patient's weight;
- weakness in any extremities or any other evidence of neuro-muscular problems;
- whether the patient has traveled in recent years, particularly to countries with indigenous diseases;
- emotional stability;
- in the case of females, history of menstruation, menopause, pregnancies, abortions, or complications.

Obviously, there is much that the careful physician needs to know about a patient. It is a time-consuming process. Some doctors believe they are knowledgeable enough to let the history-taking slide—that it is a waste of time. It is difficult in the course of a day to sit in one's office, listening to patient after patient, paying careful attention to sometimes lengthy descriptions of medical conditions. But doctors who feel that way are wrong. Failing to take a thorough history is sloppy medicine, and there is a good chance that these individuals will find themselves facing malpractice charges one day. People should choose only professionals who understand that this is not an unpleasant chore, but the key to an accurate diagnosis and the way to determine a proper course of treatment.

The next step in the visit to a doctor is the physical examination, another area where some doctors have shortcomings and patients should be on the alert. Doctors who spend a few minutes listening to their patients, then make snap diagnostic judgments based on a cursory examination are doing nothing more than educated guesswork. Patients deserve better than that.

When done properly, an examination should be done literally from top to bottom, in a systematic fashion that guards against inadvertent oversights. Most errors in the examination process occur because of carelessness and undue haste. As with histories, examination results should be written down immediately, while they are fresh in the physician's mind. If a doctor is not taking notes, he or she could well be asking for trouble. We have seen many cases where errors resulted because of a physician's sloppy practice of writing or dictating notes—notes that turned out to be inaccurate—long after the examination took place.

In brief, there are four methods of examining patients: inspection, or looking at the patient; palpation, or touching the patient; percussion, or tapping the patient; and auscultation, or listening to the patient. After taking the patient's vital signs and conducting a general inspection, the examining physician should review the patient's skin, head, eyes, ears, nose, mouth, throat and neck, chest and lungs, heart, breasts, abdomen, genitalia, extremities, back and spine, nervous system, and rectum.

The time involved in taking the medical history and performing the physical examination marks the difference between a competent, diligent physician and a negligent one. Both functions take time, and in the medical profession, as in any other, time is money. The more patients a doctor can see in a day, the more fees he will collect. That provides a great incentive for not practicing good medicine, but rather for moving patients in and out of the office as quickly as possible.

Patients should insist on doctors who are willing to devote the time necessary to practicing good medicine, not only in examinations and histories but all other aspects of the doctor-patient relationship as well. All too often doctors treat their patients as no more than objects upon whom they practice their skills. They make it clear by their demeanor that they don't like to spend time talking, that they don't like to be questioned, or that they really can't be bothered explaining themselves to the ignorant people who pay their fees.

That attitude is unconscionable. Even if the medical profession were as perfect as it wishes it were, such behavior would still be unacceptable. With hundreds of thousands of lives destroyed by medical incompetence each year, patients not only should have the right but should feel an obligation to themselves to be interested in their medical treatment. They should want to ask questions about their care and demand as much time and patience of their doctor as is necessary.

Research conducted by Dr. Richard Frankel at the University of Rochester Medical School has found that many physicians assume that the first complaint voiced by the patient is the one they should focus on, cutting off further discussion within a few minutes. But Dr. Frankel, as quoted in *The New York Times* on November 13, 1991, said, "there's no relationship between the order in which patients bring up their concerns and their medical significance. For most patients we've studied, when their physician gives them the chance to say everything on their mind, the third complaint on average is the most troubling." Unfortunately, many doctors don't let patients get that far. A 1984 study by Dr. Frankel found that fifty-one out of seventy-four patients studied, who visited internists for various medical problems, were interrupted by their physicians within only eighteen seconds of attempting to describe their complaints.

Such behavior is not only rude, it is contrary to the medical interests of patients. People generally receive better medical care and have better results when they play a more active role during the diagnostic process. Researchers at Tufts University, for example, did a study in 1989 in which they separated patients waiting to see their doctors into two groups, one of which they coached on how to ask pertinent questions and overcome their timidity in dealing with the physician. Four months later, the patients who had been coached reported that they had lost fewer days from work because of illness, had had fewer symptoms, and were generally more healthy. Patients with hypertension found that their blood pressure had gone down, and patients with diabetes found that their blood glucose levels were lower on average than those patients who had been more passive during their examinations.

Diabetes Care reported in October 1991 on another study with similar results, showing that patients who asked their doctors more questions, interrupted if necessary, and exerted more control over their medical interviews and examinations had a 15 percent drop in their blood sugar levels within two months.

Better communication between doctor and patient is of value not just to the patient but to the physician as well. According to the *New York Times* (November 13, 1991), "The research also shows that empathic doctors are generally among those most satisfied with their work, have patients who are most pleased with their medical care and are less likely than most physicians to be sued for malpractice." As in any other profession, people who take time with and show interest in their work derive the most satisfaction from it and do it best. Doctors who make an effort to treat their patients not as objects but as intelligent partners in the health-care process enjoy their work more. Their patients are more satisfied with the treatment they receive because, in fact, they receive better treatment.

It should be no surprise that conscientious physicians are involved in fewer malpractice lawsuits than their less diligent colleagues. They take more time and care with their patients, so they make fewer mistakes. Fewer mistakes means fewer unnecessary deaths, fewer avoidable injuries, and fewer lawsuits.

Obviously, having selected a physician and undergone an examination, the next step for the patient is the diagnosis and recommended course of action. A good doctor will again take time to explain as much about his or her findings and recommendations as possible. A diligent medical consumer will try to remain calm, give the matter thought, ask questions, and learn as much from the doctor as possible about his illness, rather than just accept vague generalities. Patients are entitled to know about their condition. What are the symptoms? What are the underlying causes of those symptoms? Telling a patient he has high blood pressure or anemia, for example, is not providing a full diagnosis. Are these symptoms caused by poor eating habits, a blood disorder, or genetic factors? Knowing the cause of the illness often determines the course of treatment, and patients should be included in this process.

Sometimes this is a difficult and traumatic moment. Diagnoses can be complicated. Patients can be flustered and find it difficult to compose themselves. They should not be afraid to ask the doctor to repeat the information and explain everything until they are satisfied.

If the patient has not already done so, he or she should go to the library and research the condition. It is often useful to write down questions or thoughts for later discussion. When the patient sees the doctor again, or speaks by phone, he can refer to the notes to be sure to get answers to every issue. If the physician tries to end the conversation abruptly, or indicates that he or she hasn't the time to deal with "silly questions," the patient may need to be persistent. If, finally, the doctor simply will not deal with the patient's concerns, it's time to see another doctor.

In any event, even when dealing with a physician one trusts, it is always wise to seek other medical opinions before undergoing surgery or treatment for a major illness. Even the best doctors can make honest mistakes, and in fact, the best doctors are happy to have their patients seek a second opinion. Good doctors don't feel as if the patient is insulting them or questioning their ability. They understand their patients' desire to get as much advice as possible and make the best decision. Good physicians often encourage patients to get second opinions. In fact, they usually consult with colleagues before carving their diagnosis in stone.

If a patient is not so fortunate, and is in the care of a physician who resents being questioned or who views second opinions as second-guessing and a threat to authority, the patient should end that relationship immediately. The patient should take the medical records, the X-rays, the test results—all of which the patient has paid for and is entitled to—and go to another doctor.

So much malpractice could be avoided if patients took the simple step of checking with a second physician before allowing themselves to be treated. We have discussed the tremendous number of unnecessary operations performed every day in hospitals across America. Twelve thousand patients die each year as a result of elective surgery that never needed to be performed. In the normal practice of medicine, patients and doctors should do everything possible to avoid the operating room, and physicians who seem too quick to recommend surgery should be avoided at all cost.

Patients should trust their instincts more. If a course of treatment seems wrong, maybe it is. If the medication doesn't seem to be working, or is causing side effects, maybe it was misprescribed. If pain or swelling or numbness won't go away and the doctor treats it with a cavalier "don't worry about it," maybe it is something to worry about. Patients should never sit idly by, feeling as if something is wrong but assuming they are overreacting. Doctors are not gods.

Symptoms are alarm bells. They are the body's way of telling us that something is wrong. When those alarm bells go off, we should heed them. If a doctor gives advice that doesn't sound quite right, or doesn't feel quite right, maybe it's not right. The only way to find out is to get a second opinion. It may be that the original doctor was correct all along. If that's the case, no harm has been done. But if the original doctor was incorrect, or negligent or incompetent, that second opinion could mean the difference between life and death.

A *Washington Post* editor wrote on May 12, 1992, of his experience of having his prostate cancer misdiagnosed as bladder cancer at one of the nation's most prestigious medical centers. He warned readers about the need to obtain second opinions, and the newspaper soon received letters from readers who had had similar experiences. One wrote:

> My original diagnosis was made in error. Doctors failed to communicate and were not there when I desperately needed them. I think my experience is not unusual. The doctors I had were well qualified. Judging by their diplomas and their professional associations, they have dedicated a major portion of their lives to fighting cancer. With that kind of commitment, they had to care. Somehow, along the way they lost something. Until they tap into their humanity again, their treatments will be futile.

Another told the story of his father-in-law:

> After undergoing surgery for a benign brain tumor in 1984 and again in 1985, he did well until the fall of 1990, when he began a gradual but significant decline in his mental and physical abilities. Seen over time by a neurosurgeon and neurologist at a hospital in Maryland as well as a private neurologist associated with a college in Virginia, he was told that this deterioration was due to scar tissue and nothing could be done to alleviate the symptoms. . . . We sought help from a physical therapist when we felt he could no longer move without a cane or walker. She suggested we see another neurologist. This physician immediately suspected hydrocephalus. After a routine X-ray series that confirmed this diagnosis, he underwent surgery for insertion of a shunt to relieve the pressure. To [the] advice to seek a second opinion I would add that in some cases, a third or fourth opinion may not be unreasonable. . . .

A woman wrote of what happened to her when her gynecologist referred her to a surgeon because a mammogram showed signs of calcification:

> I immediately went to a local hospital, where I was told that the mammogram I provided was not good enough to be read and would have to be retaken. Another doctor at the hospital then determined that there were no signs of "calcification" in the retaken mammogram. Needless to say, I walked around with breast cancer for nine months before discovering the lump myself. . . . My most fervent advice is that patients must be their own advocates, even in the most difficult of circumstances. No sign is too silly to follow up if it may impact a life.

As we have often seen, obtaining a second opinion can be a critical checkpoint in preventing malpractice. But this is only the case when the second physician is as thorough and careful as if the patient had never before been examined. Sometimes, when a patient seeks a second opinion the consulting physician merely reviews the records of the original doctor, accepts the original examination at face value, and assumes that all appropriate tests were performed and performed accurately. He then determines whether the original doctor's diagnosis and recommendation make sense based on that doctor's information. Often, however, it was the examination that was faulty or careless, or perhaps test results were mixed up or misread. A second opinion based on faulty data will be just as far off as the first opinion. If the second opinion is to be meaningful, the doctor who provides it must arrive at it after carefully taking the patient's history, performing an examination, and forming an independent opinion.

Once the patient's medical problem has been identified and a course of treatment determined to the patient's satisfaction, the next step often involves a stay in a hospital. This too is an important decision. If the treating physician has been selected wisely, he or she is probably affiliated with a top institution, where patients generally receive competent care. In all likelihood, that is where the treatment would take place. But even in this area, patients have a choice and they should exercise it intelligently.

While small community hospitals may be all right for certain routine procedures, it is best to use large teaching hospitals for anything major, like surgery. They are better equipped to handle emergencies, and they usually have the best, most modern facilities and most competent physicians on staff.

While it is currently impossible to obtain definitive ratings of the hospitals, consumers should make use of whatever information is available. The federal government's Health Care Financing Agency publishes annual statistics on hospital mortality rates around the country. Hospitals that do badly in this rating always argue that there were extenuating circumstances, as is mentioned in chapter 4. But if a particular hospital has a higher than average mortality rate year after year, it would be wise to ask for an explanation. Most people would probably feel more comfortable having surgery in a hospital with a low mortality rate than in one with a high rate, regardless of the explanation.

When physicians refer patients to a hospital for treatment or surgery, they rarely take these matters into account. Their natural inclination is to refer patients to the hospital with which they are affiliated, without regard for differences in quality. So it is up to patients to protect themselves. Ask the doctor why he or she recommends a particular hospital. Is it because they are particularly well qualified to handle certain types of cases? Or is it simply because it is convenient? If that hospital has been cited as having a high mortality rate, ask for an explanation. Is there a reason why the statistics are not relevant? Or hasn't he or she given it any thought?

An article in the *Wall Street Journal* (January 22, 1992) reported several pertinent examples. A study of cardiac bypass units in Chicago found that the four city hospitals with the busiest units had mortality rates averaging four times as high as four other hospitals in nearby suburbs. A study of hospitals in Maine, New Hampshire, and Vermont showed certain hospitals with mortality rates two and a half times higher than others. And one surgeon personally had a mortality rate among his patients four times higher than his counterpart with the lowest rate. Both of these studies may be disputed, of course, but they came to their conclusions after accounting for demographic and other differences that might otherwise skew the results.

The federal government's mortality-rate survey also shows a wide spread between hospitals with lowest and highest mortality rates. Available with a state-by-state breakdown and organized by type of illness, it shows, for example, that mortality rates among patients in the Washington, D.C., area undergoing hip replacement or reconstruction ranged from 0 percent in some hospitals to 16.7 percent in others. Which hospital would you want to use for a hip replacement?

Within the same community, for patients undergoing coronary bypass surgery—a procedure that has become fairly common and results in a mortality rate of approximately 4 percent nationwide—individual hospital mortality rates varied from 2.2 to 17.1 percent. Obviously, many factors may account for the difference. The hospital with the higher rate may have got more complicated cases or performed the surgery on more patients with multiple illnesses. Or it may be less competent. Patients should do what they can to gain access to this information, and should insist on an explanation from their physicians before they undergo treatment.

Even once patients have made an informed decision about a hospital and a primary physician, the job is not finished. During a hospital stay, particularly if patients are undergoing surgery, they will come into contact with a number of physicians. In the vast majority of instances, these individuals—anesthesiologists, radiologists, pathologists—are anonymous figures whose credentials patients never have an opportunity to check and whom they rarely bother to question. They often don't even realize they have been under the care of these doctors until they receive the bills from the hospital. Yet these physicians can make all the difference in a patient's treatment. A radiologist misreading an X-ray can result in disaster. A careless anesthesiologist, such as the one we described who went out to lunch during surgery, can kill a patient.

Every patient has a right to know exactly who is going to be responsible for his or her care. Patients should know the names, and have an opportunity to check the credentials, of every physician who will play a role in the treatment. To the extent that it is possible to anticipate such things, it is best to have this information in advance. Once in the hospital, while undergoing treatment, it will be much more difficult. Even then, asking a friend or family member to act as one's eyes and ears is well worthwhile.

This is one of the *many* reasons why it is wise for patients to have someone they trust with them at the hospital, looking after their interests. Making informed decisions requires a great deal of attention, and may be difficult for someone who is ill and hospitalized. Having a trusted companion—a spouse or significant other—will help. That person can question doctors, can prevent a patient from being ignored, or can catch obvious mistakes that the patient may be too weak or too flustered to notice.

It's not easy being a well-informed medical consumer. It's not easy to be a good doctor. But the stakes are high. At the end of this chapter, we have included a brief checklist that may help patients as they seek the best physicians and the best health care possible. While a checklist may be somewhat simplistic, we hope this device will at least prompt some consumers to examine the important elements of the health-care process.

Clearly, both patient and doctor need to find ways to do better. Thus far, individual physicians and their professional organizations have failed to take the necessary steps in the right direction. But the public can force the issue.

In the future, as the public and policymakers in government begin to understand the true nature of this epidemic, medical malpractice is bound to become a much larger public concern, and physicians will have no choice but to deal with it. If the profession does not heed those concerns willingly, it will be forced to by market conditions similar to those that operate in any other industry. If consumers become increasingly well informed and insist on thoughtful, careful, quality medical care, doctors will have to start providing it. At the same time, public officials will undoubtedly begin to act more responsibly to protect the public from incompetent practitioners.

If, on the other hand, the medical profession recognizes the terrible nature of this problem and takes action to reform itself, it will not only reduce malpractice litigation but cause a widespread improvement in the quality of medicine being practiced.

CHECKLIST FOR MEDICAL CONSUMERS

Finding a Doctor
1. Ask other competent doctors for referrals.
2. Do a search of professional publications for articles on related subjects to identify the experts in the field.
3. Check the physician's background before being treated, either with the office and/or in a directory at the library.
   - What medical school did the doctor attend?
   - Is the doctor board certified in his or her specialty?
   - Where did the doctor do his or her residency?
   - What hospitals, medical centers, or universities is the doctor affiliated with?
4. Ask the state health department about any disciplinary actions.
5. Do not choose a physician because of location, religion, fee, acceptance of a particular insurance plan, or publicity.

Obtaining Quality Care
1. Insist on a doctor who takes time and does not seem in a rush to the next appointment. The doctor should:
   - Take a thorough medical history.
   - Do a complete physical examination.
   - Listen patiently to what you have to say and to any questions you have.
   - Be available during off-hours in case of emergency, particularly if an obstetrician or pediatrician.

2. Do as much research as possible on your condition and don't be afraid to ask the doctor questions. Get all the information you feel you need.
3. Always get a second opinion before undergoing a major procedure.

Choosing a Hospital

1. If possible, choose large medical centers with modern facilities or hospitals affiliated with universities.
2. Select the hospital that is best to deal with your problem, not necessarily the one most convenient for the doctor.
3. Check the federal Health Care Finance Agency study of mortality rates for hospitals in your area, and question your physician if these statistics cause concern.
4. Make an effort to learn about the credentials of every doctor who will be involved in your treatment, from anesthesiologists to pathologists.

INDEX

211